FOLIE A DEUX

FOLIE A DEUX

An Experience of One-to-One Therapy

Rosie Alexander

FREE ASSOCIATION BOOKS / LONDON / NEW YORK

First published in 1995 by
Free Association Books Ltd
Omnibus Business Centre
39–41 North Road, London N7 9DP
and 70 Washington Square South
New York, NY 10012–1091

99 98 97 96 95   5 4 3 2 1

ISBN 1 85343 316 0 hardback

A CIP catalogue record for this book is available from
the British Library.

Designed, typeset and produced for Free Association Books by
Chase Production Services, Chipping Norton, OX7 5QR
Printed in the EC by The Cromwell Press, Broughton Gifford, England

Contents

Author's Note

In order to protect the identity of the people described in this book, their names and other points of identification have been changed throughout.

Readers will, of course, also appreciate that the author does not necessarily share all the views expressed in the Afterword.

Prologue

SOME YEARS AGO I started taking drugs. I did not swallow them, inject them, smoke them or sniff them. I imbibed them, unwittingly at first, through some kind of emotional osmosis in the course of therapeutic encounters.

Like their chemical counterparts, these drugs (administered by a process known as transference) turned out to be intoxicating, addictive, hallucinogenic and destructive. My dealers were respectable, middle-class professionals who meant me no harm.

This is the account of how I experienced it.

Marion

AT THE TIME I speak of I lived in Paris and was beset by a number of problems. No single one of these would have been been more than I could cope with, but their combined effect was seriously undermining me.

The company for which I worked as a technical writer had recently gone out of business, a situation in itself enough to trigger off a mid-life crisis in someone already in her early forties. As well as that, I had for a long time been bogged down in a series of complex financial problems which were now substantially exacerbated by the redundancy. And I was deprived of the crutch which had always supported me in the face of stress and anxiety as I had just given up smoking. Not only did this make it more difficult for me to look on my bleak circumstances with equanimity, I found myself increasingly unable to deal with any kind of social contrariety. Whereas previously I had subjugated all negative emotions by drawing furiously on a cigarette, I now let rip, often behaving with inappropriate and unreasonable aggressiveness. In the space of a short time I lost three close friends. Things were getting out of hand.

While in the midst of this turmoil I attended an assertiveness training workshop. The person running the workshop was a Neuro-Linguistic Programming (NLP) therapist who also offered individual therapy sessions. Marion impressed me, both as a person and professionally, so I arranged to do some work with her privately on a specific problem which was at the forefront for me at the time. I had always been incapacitated by crippling attacks of diffidence and low esteem when being interviewed for jobs and I felt that this was something I might be able to sort out with her.

I found the first session worthwhile. The technique she used – a kind of systematic approach to examining each aspect of a problem and evaluating the outcomes of the various ways of reacting to them – helped to order my thoughts in a more rational manner. As an added bonus her dynamism and enthusiasm were somehow infectious, moving me some way towards a less pessimistic outlook.

After this first positive experience I decided to continue seeing her as I felt the need for ongoing support to see me through what I was still experiencing as a very difficult period. I also felt that I could make use of this therapeutic situation to help me deal with other emotional problems which had always hampered my life. These could be summed up as a constant seesawing between behaviour which was either overly aggressive or wimpishly timid; always overshooting the acceptably assertive – a syndrome which, I gathered from the workshop I had attended, was not uncommon. So I arranged to see Marion once a week for a one-and-a-half-hour session.

A very dynamic, and for me highly-charged, relationship was quickly established between us. Strong transferential bonds had already been formed; rather incongruously as this phenomenon which is fundamental to psychoanalytic treatment has no function in many other therapies such as NLP. Increasingly, I found that I had little interest in dealing with the problems under discussion in terms of the systematic NLP approach, being drawn more and more into a powerful personal relationship with Marion herself which I felt compelled to act out.

Within a matter of weeks I had been sucked down into an emotional whirlpool with Marion – an experience which was all the more bewildering as, given my initial impression of her and my subsequent objective perceptions, it was a singularly unlikely thing to occur.

I first saw Marion as I waited for the assertiveness training workshop to begin. It was being held in an American cultural centre and was attended mostly by an assortment of diplomatic wives. Had I been asked to construct an identikit picture of the sort of person I would expect to find running a workshop of this nature I would have imagined someone youngish, hyperactive, offbeat but nevertheless 'with it'. Not so. A large, dowdy, frumpish woman in her fifties stepped out in front of us: sensible lace-up shoes; thick ribbed stockings; dull navy skirt and jumper; short, bobbed, grey hair; plain, shiny face. It was as if a Latin mistress had materialised out of the pages of a 1950s schoolgirls' story. I felt tricked, duped. How could a woman like this have anything to say which could be of any relevance to my life? How could there be any overlap between her psychological make-up and mine to make communication possible or meaningful? What could this woman know about acquiring assertiveness? She simply passed through life with all the lumbering ease of a steamroller.

She started off in a fairly conventional manner, using a flip-chart to illustrate patterns of relationships and behaviour. A strong personality quickly emerged, one which completely belied her appearance. She had soon established a dynamic rapport with the group. During the rest of the day we split up into small groups, analysing personal situations among ourselves along the lines she had indicated. At this stage in my contact with her I had the impression that I was being 'mothered', though there was nothing remarkable in

4

this. Any social relationship involves a certain amount of role-playing in which each person represents something for the other.

My first visit to her at home stimulated me in a strange and unusual way and I was impatient to see her again. I was already reacting differently to her appearance and physical presence, factors which were always to be of particular significance to me. Her figure was now statuesque, imposing and comforting. She had the most beautiful head of hair. And how could I ever have thought of this face, which radiated a kaleidoscopic range of expression, as plain and shiny?

A certain feeling of being at cross-purposes began to develop after the first couple of sessions. Marion obviously (and quite rightly, given that that was her line of business) wanted to use her NLP techniques with me. I didn't want any of that. For a start, I felt that the method was too superficial for my profoundly engrained problems, and, more importantly, I wanted to get directly and deeply involved in a psychodrama-type relationship with her.

Marion was a flexible and energetic woman. Seeing that the NLP was not going down too well she met me halfway. What this meant was that she more or less abandoned the NLP structures and we just talked; not just ordinary talking, but a kind of psychotherapeutic exchange facilitated by the fact that she had experience of a number of other therapies in addition to NLP.

This wasn't enough for me. I was by now welded to her by a visceral bond which I couldn't understand or identify and which had no parallel in my conscious experience. She became the emotional centre of gravity of my life. All my emotional energy was poured into my relationship with her. My thoughts revolved almost exclusively around our encounters – browsing over previous ones, projecting towards the next one. It was infatuation, but without sexual desire, which seemed a contradiction in terms. This of course forced me to examine very closely the nature of my feelings for her. Was it sexual attraction? Did I, so far wholly and satisfactorily heterosexual, have some remanent homosexual inclinations which had been reactivated by the very particular situation I was in? I tried to imagine doing with Marion whatever it is that lesbians do. It left me cold. I tried to imagine her wanting me to do it with her. And I felt that, in that case, I would willingly do it; not because it would be a pleasure in itself for me, but because anything I could do to please her would, by virtue of her pleasure, please me.

But this was all fantasy. A fantasy which perhaps was belied by the fact that in reality I wasn't doing anything to please her. My perceptions, judgements, emotions and reactions didn't correspond in any way to hers. So of course the way I was trying to handle the situations which were giving rise to so much angst in my life didn't meet with her approval. An element of constant tussle entered into the relationship.

The tussle was both a pain and a pleasure. It distressed me that I wasn't playing the role of the perfect child for Marion, but at the same time it allowed me to introduce conflict into our relationship, to drag this into the open, to confront each other, to have rows: in other words, to act out emotions, to express myself violently, and thus to have an intimate, rather than just a professional or conventionally social, relationship.

My feelings for Marion intensified. During the 166-and-a-half hours a week when I was not with her I thought about her constantly. The rest of my life was dwarfed into insignificance. Whether I was working, interacting with other people or engaged in any kind of activity whatsoever, a part of my mind was always reserved for her. In fact I resented all the other activities of my life as they occupied mental space which I needed in order to let this relationship flourish to the full. 'Relationship' was no longer an adequate word to describe what bound us together. In my mind, I was transported into another world where I existed in a state of rhapsodic communion with Marion. We did nothing, we said nothing, we just were.

During the remaining one-and-a-half hours of the week things were different. This period represented a kind of no-man's-land between fantasy and reality, two worlds which were never to co-exist with any degree of ease. Obviously not, as Marion did not deal in transference therapy and was becoming quite nonplussed by the turn things were taking. I, too, was rather disconcerted and bemused by what was happening to me. Not only that, I found it embarrassing because it somehow seemed indecent to be having these feelings about a woman and I wanted to hide them from Marion. So we never talked about them openly.

But they manifested themselves in a number of ways. In spite of myself, but at the same time with a kind of voluptuous willingness, I allowed myself to regress: becoming, behaving, talking, even thinking, like a very young child. Marion responded as if she was talking to an adult, as she had every right to assume. I was demanding; I was jealous of her receiving other clients. Sometimes she was still with the previous client when I arrived, a situation I couldn't tolerate. But neither of us could lay bare and deal with the underlying reason for this, which was that I wanted her all for myself, and being deprived of this made me want to fling myself down on the floor and scream myself into a state of uncontrollable fury. So I rationalised by telling her that I resented it because, as she had told me herself, she got tired if she didn't have half an hour between clients, and therefore I felt that I wasn't getting a fair deal. She went along with this specious reasoning and we both pretended that the reason for my anger was purely a practical one.

Strangely enough, I had no feelings of jealousy regarding her son, a boy of about twelve who would often come bursting into the room where Marion and I sat to speak to his mother when he got home from school. I could burn inside with rage thinking about her relationship with other clients, but the fact that this child was bound to her in the most intimate relationship of all didn't touch me.

Another source of malaise for me was that our outlooks on life were totally discordant. I didn't want to recognise this fact. I tried to fashion her according to the image that was psychologically necessary to me, and to do so I interposed a filter between us, only allowing through those things which fitted in with this image. However, this filter was very inefficient and I was aware, as if just out of the corner of my eye, of all the things I was refusing to see – not because they were faults, but because they didn't correspond with *my* notion of the ideal person; things which, from the standpoint of my austere, undemonstrative, working-class background were irredeemably bourgeois, mawkish or whimsical. I tried not to see her, even physically. Sometimes I thought she was beautiful; sometimes I thought bits of her were beautiful and I tried to see these bits and shut out the others; sometimes I thought she was frightful and I couldn't look at her at all. Normally I hated the way she dressed. It made me curdle up inside to think that my ideal person could be clothed like this.

Several times she was away for periods of a couple of weeks. On these occasions we wrote to each other. This brought me even more brutally face-to-face with the incompatibility of our minds and temperaments. When we spoke I could apply the filter, turn a deaf ear to things I didn't want to hear and distort the sense of what was said by remembering the words, the tone of voice or the facial expression differently from what they had actually been. Reading her letters I had a feeling of complete alienation, and it was inescapable. The words were there, static, in front my eyes: I could read and re-read them, but I didn't want to because they didn't convey the thoughts of the person I wanted to communicate with. Yet I still longed for her letters. Each time a letter arrived with her writing on it I pounced on it, heart pounding, desperate to know what it had to say to me. Then I would read it, elation slowly giving way to disillusionment as I realised that I couldn't relate at all to the person who had written it.

Another significant obstacle for me was that, unusually for a therapist, Marion allowed her moral judgements to enter into the therapeutic exchange, and to such an extent that she flatly refused to let me express some of my more negative feelings, thereby depriving me of very necessary space. This threw me off balance because not only did I think it was unprofessional of her, it also laid a whole new burden of guilt on me – something I was already amply laden with.

Things began to get out of hand. I was obsessed with Marion. She realised this and, not having the therapeutic tools to deal with it, had to find some other solution. So, very tactfully, she suggested that I should see a psychiatrist, who would be better equipped to work with all the primal feelings I was getting into. She already knew of one who was highly recommended by a friend of hers. I would, of course, she hastened to add, carry on seeing her as usual. There was no question of rejection.

At first I felt no particular enthusiasm. Then one day, while idly toying with the idea, I had a kind of quasi-psychedelic sensation whereby I suddenly experienced a tremendous upsurge of hate and anger which I vomited out over this psychiatrist, as yet unknown, and which brought me a glorious feeling of relief.

I phoned Dr Weissmann.

Dr Weissmann

THE ADDRESS WAS in a boringly chic part of the 14th arrondissement. I found myself in a large barn of a waiting room, furnished
indiscriminately as if several people of very different tastes had used
it as a dumping ground for things they no longer had house-room
for. Large double doors led from the waiting room into the consulting room of another doctor who shared the premises, a urologist
whose strident voice I could hear clearly as I sat waiting for half an
hour beyond the appointed time. I leafed through copies of *Elle*.

The waiting was brought to an end when a handsome man in his
mid-forties entered. 'Madame Alexander?' he enquired. I nodded and
he shook my hand. I eyed him carefully. Smart, dark blue suit,
rather glamorous but manly good looks with a striking resemblance
to Jeremy Paxman; tall, strong and very male. I was surprised. Without ever having formulated the idea consciously, I must have
assumed that all psychiatrists were old, shrivelled-up and ugly.

He took me down a long gloomy corridor to an equally gloomy
room in which I was never to feel physically comfortable. Dispropor-
tionately narrow and with an ill-chosen layout of furniture, it was
vaguely reminiscent of a railway buffet car. We sat facing each other,
cramped into a corner on two low chairs. A box of tissues had been
thoughtfully placed within reach of the patient.

Dr Weissmann lounged nonchalantly in front of me, one leg draped
elegantly over the other, and gave me a quizzical look. 'I'm listening.'

I explained what had brought me there, starting with the unmanageable emotions in real-life situations and going on to the intense
feelings about Marion which she had been unable to manage. He
prodded with the occasional question and then stopped me rather
abruptly after about twenty-five minutes. He had a train to catch, he
told me, but would like to speak to me again before deciding if he
would accept me as a patient as I had not yet satisfactorily explained
what I wanted from him. I was a bit surprised at this as I thought,
naively perhaps, that the fact of wanting to go to a psychiatrist was
evidence in itself of the need to do so. We made an appointment for
the following week. He had made no emotional impact on me of any
kind.

The next session was more or less a repetition of the first except that afterwards, as I looked back on it, I found that I was beginning to be attracted to him. But then he was attractive. Perhaps after all, I thought, only old, shrivelled-up, ugly people should be allowed to become psychiatrists, like the nuns who must be of 'canonical age' before being allowed to work in the Vatican, to avoid any possible confusion between transference and straightforward, up-front desire. In the end I decided he was quite simply fanciable; physically attractive and with a certain kind of macho, sardonic personality which a masochistic streak in me readily responded to.

I was taken on board. In response to my still ill-defined request for psychiatric treatment, he finally grudgingly admitted, 'We could perhaps go a little further.' I was to have one thirty-minute session a week.

We were soon provided with extra material to work on. The original problems which had led me to consult Marion were now virtually put in the shade by a personal catastrophe of such proportions that I was catapulted into a state of psychopathic rage and abysmal depression. A minor nose operation which I had just undergone had gone badly wrong and I was left with what to my mind was a serious disfigurement. I couldn't bear to look at myself in the mirror. I couldn't bear to look anyone in the face because I was so afraid to let them see mine. I dwelt obsessively on fantasies of taking revenge on the surgeon who had done this terrible thing to me, of throwing acid in his face, blinding him, preventing him from ever operating again. For a couple of months everything else was forgotten and the sessions revolved exclusively around this. No, 'revolved' is too dynamic a word; they stagnated, rather. Each session was a stagnant pool of negative feeling, languidly stirred from time to time by the posing of a bored question, the purulent surface occasionally disturbed as a lazily ironic comment was dropped into it.

During this time I was becoming increasingly sexually attracted to the man, but in a purely cerebral way. Being in his presence excited me and I was 'aware' of him as one is normally aware of a sexually attractive man, but I had no conscious desire for a physical relationship with him. I didn't fantasise about it. I tried to conjure up the appropriate images in my mind to see what effect it would have on me, but as soon as they formed, they simply dissolved again. It seemed to be a sexual desire which had no need of physical expression.

During the first few months the situation plunged me even further into gloom and despair. Finding someone sexually attractive is, I suppose, normally accompanied by a need for the feeling to be reciprocated. I would never have admitted it to him (pride prevented me saying a lot of things to him which should have been said), but I desperately needed to feel that he had some kind of emotional response to me as a woman. Nothing, from my pessimistic outlook at the time, could have been more unlikely.

10

Most of his other clients, as far as I could see from those I overlapped with in the waiting room, were young, trendy, rich and attractive. I felt as if, together, we formed his harem, of which I was the Cinderella.

Not only that, I just wasn't his type. Even if there hadn't been this bevy of rivals to compare me unfavourably with, he would still have remained impervious. I imagined him being attracted to large, full-bodied women, bourgeois and sensible but also sophisticated. I was the opposite: small, frail and a bit of a gypsy. And, worst of all, there was the facial disfigurement which he must surely find repellent.

'All your clients are women. Why?' I growled at him aggressively.

'Because more women than men go to psychiatrists and because I have a special rapport with women,' he replied complacently, an answer which only discouraged me further as I felt excluded from this special rapport.

I felt sexless, unseductive, unerotic.

To make matters worse, I felt that the negative feelings I was having to talk about, and the situations in my life giving rise to them, were only making things worse. It was as if I was having a vaginal infection treated by a rather dashing gynaecologist. To my mind I was an unappetising case and I envied all those other women who, I imagined, had stimulating and juicy stories to talk about, all of them involving some kind of sexual problem, I jealously assumed.

In fact, talking to him about sex was a scenario which would have excited me in a way which the thought of an actual physical relationship with him was unable to do. I wanted to have a verbal sexual relationship with him. Unfortunately, sex was one of the few areas of my life which had never presented any real problem. At that particular time it was an issue which was pretty much on the back-burner as I was in the moribund stages of a relationship with a lover I had been with for some years and we were now seeing each other less and less frequently.

In any case I felt compelled to talk to Dr Weissmann about the relationship which had begun to exist between me and him.

'Do you like me?' I asked.

'Mmm, I'm not sure,' he murmured evasively.

I was disappointed. Was he trying not to hurt my feelings? Or perhaps it was the kind of question psychiatrists didn't answer. The reply finally came out of the blue during our next session. 'I think, after all, I find you quite likeable,' he drawled, stretching his legs nonchalantly and gazing at me through half-closed eyes. 'Because of your intelligence. And there's something a bit wild about you that appeals to me.' I was gratified. 'You're a rum character,' he added, a remark which I wasn't quite sure how to take. On another occasion he told me, apropos of nothing in particular, that he thought that I must have been an impudent and tiresome child. I took this to mean that he found me an impudent and tiresome adult.

After some months I began to think that I had no further need to see him. I had managed to find another surgeon who had rectified the damage done by the first; I had started to work with a friend, Valerie, who ran a translation agency and the nicotine withdrawal symptoms had long since abated. The intense feelings I had had about Marion had gradually been extinguished during the time I had been seeing Dr Weissmann and contact between us was now reduced to the occasional phone call. So, in various ways, most of my immediate problems had been solved.

I told him I wouldn't be coming any more. We shook hands and I walked out through the long gloomy corridor for the last time.

I think I knew from the beginning that I was deluding myself, playing a charade. For the first couple of days I was fretful. By the third day I knew it was only a question of time, of seeing how long I could hold out. On the fifth day I phoned him. I was given my usual appointment for the following week.

Everything peripheral to the relationship existing between him and me had now been shed. It was direct confrontation: I attacked him; accused him of being conceited, smug, arrogant, cocksure and vain; vilified him for a multiplicity of faults; abused him; insulted him. It all amounted to saying one thing: 'You think you're God's gift both to women and to mankind; I think you're an arsehole, but I need you, I'm addicted to you, I can't do without you.' He sat looking mildly attentive, taking no exception to my words.

'Things are becoming more interesting now,' he said, rising to indicate that my thirty minutes were up. I wrote him a cheque and we shook hands.

The relationship had moved from first to second gear. It was never to develop any further. The pattern had now been set for our mode of communication during the rest of our time together. I settled into it as into an uncomfortable rut.

At times I thoroughly disliked him, thinking he was a prat, a swank and an idiot. I resented the state of emotional subjection which bound me to this strutting peacock. I never felt any warmth or affection for him. But I did get pleasure out of the verbal skirmishing, outwitting him or, more rarely, being outwitted by him, which gave me an even greater thrill. And all the time there was the ill-defined, out of focus, desire for him and the desire to be desired by him.

The frustration of these desires made me aggressive. 'You fancy yourself as a ladykiller? All these women who come to see you, they're in love with you, I suppose. That's why you're a psychiatrist, because that sort of thing turns you on, you get a kick out of thinking that they fantasise about your being their lover?'

'Not at all. I represent a lot of different things for my patients.'

'What, for example?' I snarled sceptically.

'Oh, I can be a brother, a sister, a father, a grandmother. Yes, in fact, I'm often a grandmother.'

'Well, for me you're a sex object. Only that. Do you understand what I mean?'

'Yes, of course. And it's true that I attract certain women.'

'I'm not talking about attraction. The emphasis is on the word "object". For me you don't have any personal value or qualities. You're just an object, but an object which excites me sexually.'

This theme, although it came up repeatedly, was never really explored any further than this. But it proved to be the final kiss of death for my relationship with Gilles, my lover, who found that he could no longer kindle any spark of sexual desire in me.

'What's wrong?' he asked, as I pushed his hands away. I told him in a confused and garbled fashion about Dr Weissmann, without fully understanding myself what I was saying. All I knew was that these strange and indistinct feelings triggered off by the therapist precluded sexual attraction to any other man.

Gilles was angrily aghast.

'But this is all madness, Rosie. And I'm surprised at you. I would have thought you were too rational, too reasonable, to be taken in by this sort of nonsense. Psychotherapy! It's an out-and-out racket; emotional swindling. Freud, indeed! That man's the conman of the century.'

We never saw each other again.

A constant source of grievance for me with Dr Weissmann was the fact that the sessions seemed to be of variable length – depending on the person, that is. I naturally suspected him of spending more time with those people (women, of course) whom he was more interested in.

I tackled him about it.

'You spend more time with the women you find attractive. With me it's barely half an hour. Last week there was a woman who stayed a whole hour with you. And I'm subsidising these people. If it's the same price for everyone then I'm paying for part of the time that you're spending with them. You're just taking advantage of me. And what do you expect me to be able to say to you in just half an hour?'

'It's true that I work on the basis of half-hour units but it sometimes happens that I keep someone for longer. It depends also on what the person can put up with. Sometimes a session only lasts ten minutes.'

I wasn't satisfied by this answer. I wanted to be the person who was kept for an hour. I had in fact noticed on one occasion that someone had stayed only ten minutes, a man I had seen in the waiting room several times; a mournful, dejected-looking creature. I felt sorry for him but thought he must be very trying as a patient, which only confirmed my suspicion that the tiresome ones were quickly dispatched.

I also resented the intrusion of the telephone which normally rang once or twice per session, stealing precious, already scarce, minutes. Not only that, its irruption annihilated whatever emotional climate was reigning at the time. When we resumed our conversation afterwards, even if I could remember what we had been saying, I was unable to reconstitute the frame of mind in which I'd been saying it. It had gone as irrevocably as a dream is lost on wakening.

I told him so.

'It annoys me that you answer the phone when I'm here. I pay you for half an hour of your time so I think you should be available to me for that length of time.' I spoke in a surly tone, expecting to be told that it was a matter of professional necessity and that I could like it or lump it.

He got up, switched the phone over to the answering machine, and sat down again with an ingenuous look on his face. This took the wind out of my sails. I had been expecting my complaint to be the first move in a prolonged battle. All the arguments I had been marshalling in support of my view were suddenly rendered redundant.

The following week the phone rang as it normally did. I said nothing and he answered it.

Several weeks later he was running even later than usual. I had already spent an hour in the waiting room and was just in the middle of my first sentence when the phone quietly warbled. He answered: he spoke at length; the conversation showed no sign of coming to a close. I simmered, then I raged. Hadn't he heard what I'd said to him a month ago? Was he deaf? Did words have no meaning? *Did the guy ever listen to anything?*

At an acme of frustration I took off my shoe and hurled it across the desk in front of him with all my might.

It hit a beautiful, antique, porcelain lamp, delicately coloured and with a fragile glass shade. The lamp toppled over.

I felt a chill dread. I knew I'd gone too far. He put the phone down and stood towering over me. 'Get out!' he shouted.

I quaked wretchedly. 'I'm sorry,' I whispered. I didn't move. He glowered at me indecisively, not knowing what to do. If he wanted rid of me he was going to have to carry me out, and in the meantime the person he had been talking to was still on the other end of the line. He decided to deal with that first and expeditiously brought the call to an end. Then he turned his attention to the lamp. Miraculously and mercifully it was unharmed. He righted it reverentially.

'Of all the things in this room it's the only one that's irreplaceable and you had to choose it. It's totally unacceptable. We're here to talk and not to act. You can't allow yourself to behave like that.

14

I'm not going to accept it. You can go and see someone else. This just isn't on.' He glared, expecting me to get up and leave.

I cowered in the chair. What he was saying seemed unjust. I hadn't 'chosen' the lamp, hadn't even seen the damn thing. It was an accident. And if we were there to talk and not to act, why the hell didn't he hear anything?

'I need you,' I whimpered, melodramatically pitiful and at the same time despising myself for it. He looked uncertain. I knew I'd won; that I wasn't going to be flung out. A few more words were exchanged. Although by no means mollified, he was already beginning to regret his violent reaction. Still cross and peevish, he finally said that I could come back again the following week, but that for the moment he'd had enough. In the circumstances it wasn't possible to have our usual session. I realised I would have to be content with that and perhaps, after all, I'd got off lightly. I slunk off down the corridor.

I often wondered what the point of it all was. Our sado-masochistic relationship was a source of pleasure to me. It introduced a vein of excitement into my life. But one doesn't go to a doctor for those reasons. Wasn't it supposed to result in something, to have some kind of beneficial effect? Perhaps I wasn't communicating with him in the way I should. But I could only communicate to him what I was already thinking or feeling, the things that were uppermost in my mind.

So I decided I would try to have other thoughts and feelings when I was with him. To do so I got drunk.

It happened almost by accident. I had an appointment with him in the afternoon of a day on which I had been invited to a Christmas lunch. This lunch was a traditional, long drawn-out French affair. It started at 11.30 a.m. and continued until about 4 p.m.: kir for the aperitif; white wine with the starter; a *trou normand* tossed down to cleanse the palate before going on to the main course; red wine; more red wine; champagne with the dessert; brandy.

I drank more than was good for me, egged on by the realisation that this was my opportunity. The nature of my relationship with Dr Weissmann was going to change that evening. At the thought of this I drank even more, like an adolescent who had decided, gritting her teeth, that she was just about to give up her virginity.

I left the restaurant and set off for my appointment. When I arrived at Montparnasse I staggered out of the metro station into the cafe opposite and vomited in the toilet. The wine had been of dubious quality. I made my way to the flat, collapsed in the waiting room, then stumbled to the toilet and again retched violently. The mixture of drinks had been lethal. And what had they made the kir with? Vinegar? I slumped back into the chair in the waiting room. When he came for me I tried to steady myself. He followed me grimly as I reeled down the long gloomy corridor.

15

'I've been drinking,' I announced to him, half triumphantly, half fearfully. Triumphant because I'd found the key to our real relationship, the one we ought to have been having all along. I had put it in the lock and I was just about to turn it. Fearful because he might disapprove. Women shouldn't get drunk.

'Why?'

It was only one word, but the tone of voice conveyed to me that I had done wrong.

I mumbled an explanation about the Christmas lunch. The rest, everything which was to have been said to him, crumbled to ashes in my mouth.

I felt dizzy. I was unable to focus my mind on anything long enough to construct a sentence about it. Fifteen embarrassing minutes dragged by.

'I've had enough,' he snapped suddenly, jumping up out of his chair. We made an appointment for the following week. I went home, sobered myself up with a bag of peanuts and pondered my failed attempt to establish contact with Dr Weissmann.

He explained the next time we met that he didn't find it useful to communicate with a patient under the influence of alcohol. One of the house rules was that the patient should present himself sober. Fair enough, I thought, but shouldn't he have been curious about my reason for feeling that I needed to get drunk? I didn't broach the question of my own accord.

We carried on this relationship, essentially one of foreplay, for about another six months. I continued to feel excited, dominated and demoralised by it. But the superficiality of the relationship, as a therapeutic one, was clearly indicated by the fact that although my mother died during the period I was seeing him, we never discussed it. I felt that it would be an affront to my mother to talk about her with this man.

I knew that I had only a limited time left with Dr Weissmann, as it had been arranged that the agency I now worked for would subcontract me for a year to a company operating in francophone Africa. As the time for this drew near I thought increasingly about the relationship, trying to analyse it and to identify in what way it had been so unsatisfactory.

I tried to discuss with him the reasons for what I felt to be a failed therapy. He said that he had found me a difficult case to deal with and that, in particular, I had not revealed my fantasies to him. I didn't know what he was talking about. What fantasies? I didn't have any.

He then went on holiday for a month. I was to see him just once more after he came back. During this time I thought a lot about the impending rupture and was surprised to discover the extent of my feelings. I expressed them in a letter to him, probably my only wholly honest and revealing communication with him.

I began aggressively:

You told me, rather belatedly, that the purpose of our meetings was to allow me to express my fantasies. Perhaps I can do so now. My current fantasy is of me screaming 'I've won, you bastard,' as I grind my heel into your face.

I say 'I've won' because I haven't revealed anything of myself to you, nothing of importance at any rate. This is a Pyrrhic victory, of course. It means that I've squandered an opportunity which, in retrospect, I feel I could have made into a truly cathartic experience.

It could have been so because I'm ripe for it now, like a boil just ready to burst.

But you've slipped through my fingers; or, more probably, you just didn't want to make yourself available in the first place. Whatever the reason, the rage I feel at being deprived of this experience is the dreadful, ineffable fury of a child being wrenched from the womb, in this case a womb of hate, before term.

And I don't know how to cope with this rage, how to express it, what to do with it. There's no way now in which I can deal with my negative feelings about you. They'll stay with me like an emotional cancer which will just grow and grow till it destroys me.

I suppose this, too, is all just fantasy. In reality, I neither like nor dislike you. If I knew you in other circumstances I would quite simply have nothing to say to you. To me you're just another bourgeois suburbanite.

So it's all the more surprising that I should find you sexually attractive. Throughout the time I've known you I've been increasingly in a state of sexual arousal. The object of all this excitement is a disembodied set of sexual organs, like those plastic items displayed in sex shops – but I know it's you.

Anyway, I'm in a dreadful mess, as if you'd picked me up, smashed me on the floor and hadn't bothered to put me together again. It makes me wonder if you can have any conception of the emotional maelstrom stirred up by 'therapy'. But this is an otiose question; of course you do.

And I ended on a pleading note:

I need to know why you played it the way you did. I want you to explain this to me. It's the only thing that can help.

The last session was an anticlimax. He explained to me that he had, in fact, kept things at a fairly superficial level deliberately, not wanting me to get into anything profound as he thought that I was too fragile to cope with it.

I felt rather flat as I walked down the corridor for the last time.

17

Luc

THE FOLLOWING DAY I awoke with the feeling that my whole emotional structure had fallen apart; the scaffolding had been removed, the very skeleton had disintegrated.

I was due to leave for Africa in five days. I had to hang on till then. Once I had left Paris, put myself beyond the orbit of desire, I would be out of his reach. My psyche would return to normal, or so I told myself.

Throughout the morning I dissolved gradually into a state of panic-stricken emotional helplessness.

It was August, the month of annual holiday, when Paris goes into purdah; doors barred, shutters closed, streets semi-silent. Not a plumber, nor a dentist, nor a cobbler to be had.

A few days previously, while idly leafing through a magazine, I had noticed a list of addresses and telephone numbers which, during this general state of dearth, could still be relied on to provide services. I remembered one by which a psychiatric service could be contacted in the event of an unseasonal fit of depression. I recalled the number without difficulty. It was an easy number to remember, being composed mainly of threes, but perhaps I had also made a subconscious note of it.

I called the number and a woman answered. We spoke briefly about my reason for calling and she said that a psychiatrist would telephone me back shortly.

The phone rang.

'*Je suis le docteur Landau. Vous avez appelé le service X, je crois?*'

'*Oui.*'

'Can you tell me what the problem is?'

I tried, inadequately, to summarise the situation.

'Would you like to come and see me?'

'Yes.'

He gave me his address and I arranged to be there in half an hour.

The crushing burden of emotional rubble suddenly felt just a little bit lighter. I was going to be able to talk to someone about it.

I arrived at the flat at the same time as a delivery boy. A small, thin, dark, very young man opened the door. He showed me into his office and left me there while he returned to deal with the delivery

19

boy. I was disconcerted. How was it possible for a psychiatrist to be so young? This one was barely more than a youth. What could he know about anything? Only adults can understand problems. Then, after the initial surprise, I realised that I didn't really care. All I needed was someone to listen to me, to provide an outlet for the build-up of all this negative emotional energy which was so under-mining me.

He came in and sat down opposite me. I stared at him through tears, unable to marshal any thoughts together.

'Would you like me to ask you some questions?' he asked, quietly, gently, solicitously.

'Yes,' I gasped gratefully. Starting on the basis of what I had already told him on the phone, he gradually led me into telling him what it was all about. We spoke for an hour. He was easy to talk to. He seemed to listen, to care.

At the end he suggested that I should come again the following day. What blessed relief! Not only had I begun to talk about it, I was going to be able to go on talking about it. I looked at him more closely, able to notice his physical presence now that I'd become a little less obsessively introspective. There was something very asexual about him. I vaguely wondered how he could kindle desire in any woman.

The next day we talked for another hour. How different it was from the sessions with Dr Weissmann. No skirmishing, no struggle to outwit the other, just an easy communication.

Later that day I learned that my departure for Africa was to be postponed until ten days after the original date. I was elated. I'd been reprieved. The few days left to me before I had expected to leave had seemed so impossibly short for everything I had to offload with Luc.

The following day when I saw him I was joyful. 'I'm not leaving on Tuesday,' I told him excitedly. I somehow felt that he was al-most as pleased as I was.

With two whole weeks now lying in front of us the pressure was off, the horizon distanced. I no longer felt that I had to unpack my mind pell-mell, seizing everything relating to Dr Weissmann and flinging it out. In particular, I began to relate to the man in front of me, though we still talked mostly of the other.

'What do you want from Dr Weissmann?' he asked, using the present tense as if there was still a possibility of my getting some-thing from him.

'I want him to look after me,' I whined childishly (admitting something which I would always have refused to recognise before).

'I think you feel a very great need for someone to look after you.'

'Yes.' As I said this I realised that the 'someone' was no longer necessarily Dr Weissmann, that it could equally well be the person I was having this conversation with. A whole new area of emotional quicksands was opening up before me.

I began to take a greater interest in him and his environment. Apart from a certain feeling of being ill at ease with his body which he seemed to radiate, he was really rather aesthetic in a small, dark, Italianate way: quite elegant; refined, intelligent.

The room we were in felt good. Nicely proportioned for the purpose, comfortable grey leather armchairs, a blue velvet couch to be used by those with whom he really got down to business, masses of books lining the shelves, a desk strewn with papers, odds and ends, bits and pieces. Unlike Dr Weissmann's little mausoleum of a room, this was a living, organic habitat.

During the following week I had four appointments. On one of these occasions he was still with another client when I arrived – the first time that this had happened. He showed me into the waiting room. I looked around. No, it wasn't a waiting room, it was a sitting room. He lived there, in that flat. I was surprised and intrigued. Psychiatrists are usually such mysterious characters to their patients but this one was revealing himself by allowing me to enter his home territory.

I took a closer look around. There was a certain higgledy-piggledy air about the place and it was somehow incomplete, as if he had only recently moved in.

There was an impression of affluence. I was in a spacious, irregularly shaped room in an area where property prices were high. Four tall windows looked out over a classical Parisian scene. To sit, there was a choice of several capacious couches, all in luxuriously soft grey leather. A thickly-tufted grey and white patterned rug covered most of the floor. Piles of compact discs littered the shelves. I longed to rummage through them to find out what kind of music he liked but was afraid of him catching me in the act of such unseemly nosiness.

I turned my attention to the walls and discovered several vividly striking abstract paintings, strong shades of dark blue predominating, with streaks of scarlet and dashes of lighter colour. One, half-finished, was propped on an easel in a corner.

He showed out the previous client. It was strange to think of him in that room with someone else. So far it had been as if I was the only one, a privileged position due to the fact that it was the month of August.

I was still concerned about his age. In fact, the more I became aware of him as a person with whom I was becoming actively involved in a dependent relationship, the more incongruous his boyishness seemed.

'You're very young,' I said. 'How old are you?'

He looked at me, silent. Psychiatrists don't answer personal questions.

'But how can you be a psychiatrist – or a psychoanalyst or whatever you are – already?' I persisted. 'You look as if you're only about twenty-seven.'

This supposition galvanised him into a denial. After all, he wanted to be taken seriously.

'Oh no, I'm not as young as all that.' He paused. 'I'm thirty-one.'

Thirty-one. Twelve years younger than me. It still seemed incongruous. How could I have a therapeutic relationship, with its preponderant parent–child element, with someone so much younger than me? I put the question to him.

'It's of no importance. My actual person doesn't count in all this. I can represent your father, your mother, or anything else at all. It doesn't matter.'

Perhaps he was right. I wanted to think so, at any rate. He was so adorable, so nice, so understanding.

I pursued my enquiries. 'And what are you? A psychiatrist or a psychoanalyst?'

'I'm a qualified medical doctor, specialising in psychiatry and attached to a psychiatric hospital. I'm also a psychoanalyst and have undergone a training analysis myself. With my patients here I practise psychoanalysis and psychotherapy.' His eyes roamed over the couch. He had presented his credentials.

I asked what his particular line of attack was. Psychotherapeutic work embraces so many isms, acronyms and schools of thought; I wanted to know which one in particular I was dealing with.

'Classical,' he replied.

'Freud, you mean?'

'Who else is there?' he asked rhetorically, with a dismissive wave of the hand, and somehow implying a kind of blind allegiance.

I was wary. Hadn't Freud's theories been developed, refined, modified, since they were first conceived about a hundred years ago? If psychoanalysis was to be considered, however loosely, as a science, this was necessarily so. In any case, *différents temps, différents moeurs*. Yet here was Luc referring to him as if he was some kind of guru. But I didn't care. It didn't matter what he thought, I only wanted him to *be*.

We talked some more about Dr Weissmann, dwelling on my jealousy and feelings of inferiority in relation to his other clients. I told him about the phone, the intolerable intrusion that it had represented and the source of conflict it had been between us. Luc's phone would occasionally ring too, but he answered it so briefly and discreetly that I barely minded. I described the incident which had resulted in the lamp being knocked over. I still felt sore about it and needed reassurance that I had been badly treated.

'I know I shouldn't have done it, that it was a bit extreme, but it was his own fault really because he'd pushed me too far. And I

22

didn't mean to knock the lamp over, I hadn't even seen it. I'm not very observant, you know. I hadn't ever noticed that there was a lamp on the table.'

'I don't agree. I think you had noticed it. And it wasn't by chance that your shoe hit it. A lamp is a very feminine object and according to what you say it was a very beautiful lamp. I think you wanted to break it. For you it represented a feminine presence. It represented all these attractive elegant women you'd seen in the waiting room and were jealous of. It was an opportunity for you to attack them.'

This interpretation seemed to me very far-fetched. I was unimpressed but I tolerated it. I couldn't expect our ideas to be in total harmony.

We talked more generally about my rupture with Dr Weissmann and the intensity of my feelings subsequent to leaving him which had taken me completely by surprise. I had had no idea that I was so dependent on him. I tried to be objective.

'After all, he's just a guy like any other.'

He smiled in amused agreement.

But the truth was that it was now much easier to be objective about Dr Weissmann because I was becoming so subjective about Luc.

By the end of the second week I was besotted with him. By this time Dr Weissmann was no more than a name from the past.

It was as if the seeds of dependence which had been sown in me by my relationships with Dr Weissmann and Marion – producing stunted growths which were to be uprooted, wither and die – had flourished, springing into glorious bloom, in the hothouse conditions of my relationship with Luc.

A number of circumstances had probably conspired to create these conditions. I was seeing him every other day, sometimes more often, for sessions of an hour which was an unwonted luxury after the thirty minutes granted parsimoniously by Dr Weissmann. I rarely saw another client, which allowed me to entertain a certain feeling of being unique. Most of all, I felt the object of undue care and attention. Luc was just setting his practice up at the time and was presumably full of enthusiasm and energy for his work. This energy and enthusiasm were readily channelled into my particular case as there were few other clients around at the time. And finally, I think he really liked me.

It was now only a few days before I was due to leave.

We no longer spoke about Dr Weissmann. We spoke about other things: certain negative feelings I had about going to Africa and the usual problems associated with being too aggressive or too timid. I hadn't yet revealed to him, overtly at any rate, my feelings about him. Nevertheless, the air was thick with my desire for him. It hung about us, tangible, like incense.

'If I wasn't going away I'd stay with you,' I said hesitantly.

'You'd stay with me.' He repeated my words gently as if he was touched by what I had said.

Nothing was said for a while.

'With Dr Weissmann I only wanted his body, but you, I want all of you.'

As I said this it seemed like the most intimate thing I had ever communicated to anyone.

At the time it seemed to express what I meant. In retrospect, it wasn't quite that, because after all I had never actually wanted Dr Weissmann's body. What I really meant was that in my relationship with him I had only been aware of being attracted by the outward manifestations of his masculinity and his personality. With Luc I wanted to possess and merge with the very essence of his being.

Despite my feelings for Luc I had never considered giving up the contract in Africa in order to stay in France and undertake some sort of therapy with him. In any case, I knew my absence was to be temporary and, although I knew that things could change a lot in a year, I told myself that I would simply start up with him again on my return – if I still felt that I wanted to.

It took me about twelve minutes to walk from my flat to his. The route was one which I had often taken in the past. It was a main artery which led to the market I used, to restaurants and cinemas. I wondered how I could have been so crassly insensible as to have walked down this road so many times before with no presage of where it would one day lead me.

I walked down it for our last appointment the day before I was to leave. We talked a lot about the impending separation. Strangely enough, it was easier than leaving Dr Weissmann. There were two reasons for this. As my relationship with Dr Weissmann was obviously a cul-de-sac, there had never been any question of going back to him when I returned to Paris. The separation was therefore final, no matter how difficult that was to accept emotionally. Secondly, perhaps irrationally, I felt that I'd failed in my relationship with Dr Weissmann, that it was my fault that nothing had come of it, and the fact that it had come to an end meant that I'd been rejected, found wanting.

I stayed with Luc for a bitter-sweet hour and a quarter. It was inconceivable that, the day after tomorrow, I wouldn't be here again as usual. I would be in Africa.

We were like lovers who had decided, heroically, to leave each other because of some force majeure, perhaps because one was married, or because they belonged to different religions, or for some other ineluctable reason.

Finally, it was time to go.

'I'm able to leave you because I know that you're not abandoning me,' I told him, alluding to my feelings about leaving Dr Weissmann.

24

'No, I'm not abandoning you.'
What did he mean, I wondered.
There was a short and rather tense silence.
He said, 'You can write to me.'
He showed me to the door.

HE'D THROWN ME a lifeline. 'You can write to me.' I rejoiced in the
idea of being able to write to him, maintaining some kind of tenu-
ous contact from the other side of the world. No matter what
happened, or how I felt, I'd be able to tell him about it. Why had
he said it? Did therapists normally propose such a thing to their
patients, especially after such brief acquaintance? Was it a kindness,
or did he think I was an interesting case who might provide him
with some entertaining correspondence?

The separation was relatively easy at first. Not only did I have the
words 'You can write to me' echoing constantly and comfortingly in
my head, but the experience of being whisked off to another conti-
nent and plunged into the Third World absorbed most of my mental
and emotional energy. In fact, I didn't even think about Luc very
much in the beginning. My mind was constantly taken up with
absorbing the sights, sounds and experiences of a world which
seemed totally alien to the one I had always known.

I was living in what was, in comparison with everything I was
used to, a city of poverty, dirt and dilapidation: tumbledown buildings; cratered road surfaces resembling a lunar landscape; shops sell-
ing only the shoddiest of goods; sleazy eating places; lepers lying
begging in the street; whole families living, cooking and sleeping on
the pavements. My first impressions were of a most unlovely place. I
hadn't known that such awfulness existed.

On the other hand, the local people were gracious and delightful,
laid back and unruffled. I felt that contact with them could do me
nothing but good, a kind of balm to the soul. Exposure to them and
their carefree philosophy would surely bring about a permanent and
positive shift in my own outlook. So Luc was relegated to a position
of lesser importance for a while, although never forgotten, and never
anything other than an object of desire.

A couple of months later my view of things had changed rather.
The city was no longer a terrible dump. In fact I'd become quite
attached to it. The gently decaying buildings gave it a romantically
old colonial air and some of the indigenous housing was really quite
splendid. The streets were lively with colourfully clad women floating gracefully along, street-vendors frying cassava or sweet potato in
gigantic pans of sizzling oil, and garishly-painted battered old buses
rattling across town, crammed to the gunnels, with heads and arms
protruding from every window.

The people were as charming as ever but I was discovering that wherever you go, you take yourself with you. In a different way, I felt just as alienated as I had always done in my own part of the world and I was having just as many difficulties there as I had had elsewhere. The more I became aware of this the more my thoughts turned to Luc and I began to suffer terribly from the idea of the distance that separated us. What a luxury it would be if I could only pick up the phone, make an appointment and go along to see him the next day. As this was impossible I would just have to write to him as he had suggested that I do.

I began to spend a lot of time thinking about what I would say in the letter. It was very difficult. I simply couldn't think of anything. If I had been able to see him I would have been able to communicate what I felt, but putting it down on paper was a different matter. I had to write something though. My feeling of isolation was now such that I desperately needed to establish intimate contact with someone. What I actually wrote was not so important. The main thing was to begin building some kind of bridge of communication. I finally sent him a short note on a beautifully hand-painted card depicting two African women pounding maize. The nice card would make up for the brevity of the words I thought. It was a kind of present which would let him know how important he was to me.

I need you. Apart from that I don't know what to say. That's my problem, I don't know what to say to anyone at all.

When I dropped the card into the letter box I felt a bit like a person marooned on a desert island tossing a bottle containing a message into the sea. Yet I never really doubted that I would get a reply. It was so obviously a cry for help.

I knew it took a minimum of one week for letters to travel to Europe. That meant I had to wait at least two weeks, probably more, before I could begin to expect an answer. After two weeks I started going to the post office every day to check my mailbox. It was usually empty. When it wasn't I would excitedly seize the letter which was lying there, and each time my heart would sink as I saw that it didn't have a French stamp, or that the writing was one I already knew. The local postal system was notoriously erratic so I didn't give up hope for a long time. It was not unknown for letters to take two months to arrive. Sometimes they didn't arrive at all.

After three months I no longer deluded myself that I was going to hear from him. I never believed at any time that this was due to a letter getting lost in the mail. I knew that my letter had arrived in Paris and that he hadn't replied to it. There must be some reason for this and I had to know what it was. It wasn't possible that he had simply decided to ignore my letter. I thought of phoning him but this was totally impractical. I didn't have a phone in my house so I would have had to go to friends, and what I had to say was far too intimate to say within earshot of anyone else. In any case, to call Europe you had to go through the operator and there was usually a delay of several hours before you finally got through. You had to tell the operator in advance how long you wanted to speak for and at the end of that time you were summarily cut off without warning. I couldn't speak to Luc in these conditions, and there was always the risk that I would end up talking to his answering machine or disturbing him while he was with a patient. So I abandoned the idea. Instead I decided to write to him again. This time I asked him specific questions so that he couldn't assume that I was just dropping him a line to let him know how I was as he may have done with the first letter.

I will be on holiday in March and am thinking of coming back to France then as I want to see you. Will you be available then?
I wrote to you three months ago. Why didn't you reply?

Two months later I had received no answer still. I was frantic. I wrote again.

I will be coming to Paris in the middle of March. It's as if I had strayed too close to a black hole and was captured by its gravitational field. I can't continue travelling on.

A couple of weeks later I flew back to Paris.

WHEN THE PLANE touched down at Charles de Gaulle airport it was as if I was coming home. How could this be so? I had never before felt that Paris was in any way my home.

The difference now was that I was coming back to Luc, to throw myself into the arms of my father/lover, to retie the umbilical cord with my mother.

Would he let me? This question didn't really trouble me – he would have no choice.

I waited a few hours before calling him. For the first time in nine months I could simply pick up a phone and speak to him. This gave me a sense of freedom which, after a while, there seemed no point in prolonging.

'Hello.'

'I'd like to speak to Dr Landau, please,' I said, not sure if it was him. Perhaps his calls were now bypassed to an answering service.

'Is that Karen?', the voice enquired, in gentle, honeyed tones – *his* voice.

It shattered me. Not only had he not recognised my voice, despite my letter telling him I would be arriving shortly, but he was letting me witness the intimacy of his relationship with someone else. Clearly, I wasn't the only person to whom kindly, considerate attention was given. Of course, I knew this, but I didn't want to be given concrete proof of it.

'No,' I muttered miserably, 'it's Rosie Alexander. I want to see you.'

'Are you in Paris?'

'Yes.'

'Can you come tomorrow morning at eleven o'clock?'

'Yes.'

'OK, I'll see you tomorrow then.'

By the following morning I had recovered somewhat from the phone call. I walked slowly down the road to his flat, feeling unreal – remembering how often I had imagined this moment while still in Africa and unable to believe that it was now happening.

We met briefly as he opened the door for me. Then he returned to the client he was already with. I had had a fleeting glimpse only, but he looked different. Features less refined, a more ordinary person than the one which existed in my memory.

I sat down on the grey leather sofa. The room no longer had the naked, just-moved-in look of the previous year. It had filled out, taken on a slightly different character. It was lived in and, I thought with a certain prurient anticipation, would yield up even more information about his personality.

Several books lay on the coffee table. A newspaper. (So he read *Libération*. But of course he would.) A medical review, still in its postal wrapper. An empty cola can. An overflowing ashtray. A vase of withering flowers.

I examined his paintings – the ones he'd done – more closely. I liked them. They were strong, powerful, colourful; the kind of work I felt I would produce myself if I could paint. Strange that I should think this as I had never had any inclination to do so. I suppose they must have been the expression of something with which I empathised.

Then, glancing into a corner, I saw a gilt and mahogany bar curving out from the wall, with two matching stools teetering on long legs. I froze with horror. It was the ultimate in kitsch. I couldn't believe – I refused to accept – that the person who represented the focus of my emotional existence could be guilty of such bad taste. I turned my back on it. From that moment on, I was always to feel threatened as I waited in that room, afraid of what I might see, of the private life that might be revealed. I had been so curious and now I realised that there could be so many things that I wouldn't want to know.

He came for me, looking, I thought, a shade uneasy, unsmiling, a cigarette already between his lips.

We sat down facing each other.

'Did you get my last letter? You knew I was coming?'

'Yes.'

'I thought you would refuse to see me.'

'But of course not. Why should I?'

'Because you didn't reply to the letters I sent you. I thought you didn't want me any more. But anyway, even if you'd told me that you couldn't see me I'd still have come. And if you hadn't let me in I'd have battered the door down. Why didn't you answer my letters?' I spoke with surly aggressiveness. Already the tone of our conversation seemed to be the antithesis of our previous way of communicating.

He replied that there had not been enough material in my first letter for him to reply to, that he had assumed it to be rather in the nature of a card on which I'd scribbled a few words.

We quibbled about this for a while, then I threw in my trump card: 'But the second letter, I sent it to ask you a specific question and you didn't reply. Why not?'

He said that he'd expected that I would phone him in order to get his reply. This struck me as being a flimsy and most unlikely excuse.

I felt outraged, but didn't dare give vent to my feelings. The relationship with him, after such a long absence and with so many new negative factors, was so fragile that there was a risk of doing it irreparable damage.

The conversation led nowhere, a fruitless exchange of accusations and excuses. Tiring of this, I moved on to the next sore point.

'When I called you yesterday, you asked if I was Karen. You can't do that sort of thing with your patients. It's too upsetting. I was devastated. You should wait to find out who's talking instead of playing guessing games.'

'It so happens that I have a Danish patient who has exactly the same accent as you. I thought it was her.'

'You were very indiscreet.'

'Yes, you're right. It was indiscreet.'

There was something unsatisfactory and disappointing about it all. He was no longer the same person and the relationship had changed. But, inexplicably, my feelings were as intense as ever.

I saw him regularly during the month I spent in Paris. The relationship shifted and changed course. We became more locked into each other, like fighting stags with their horns intertwined, a significant difference from the previous situation in which I had passively adored him. It was agreed that I would commit myself to ongoing therapy with him when I finally returned to France (though neither the nature of this therapy nor the reasons for it were ever clearly defined).

But it was a relationship riddled with cancer. I knew that he'd behaved badly over the letters. He'd done wrong – both professionally and at a personal level. In a way it was understandable, the kind of thing that happens all the time in non-therapy situations. You offer to do something because you're a nice person, or because the circumstances seem to call for it at the time, or some such reason. Then, some time later, 'out of sight, out of mind'; anyway you really can't be bothered, and in any case the person probably hadn't taken you seriously.

Only this wasn't a non-therapy situation.

It had rocked me to the emotional foundations. And not only had I suffered the actual rejection and the pain of being abandoned, but the newly re-established relationship still risked being jeopardised by this treachery. How could I entrust my 'self', entering into a state of total vulnerability, to the person who'd done this to me?

The answer was that I didn't have any choice. I don't think I would even have wanted a choice. All I wanted was him.

WHEN I FINALLY returned from Africa three months later I felt full and ripe. I phoned him and made an appointment as soon as I got back. I was going to deliver myself to him. Although I had seen him so many times before, the next session would be the consummation of our relationship.

For the past year I had desired him wholly, but with a desire that was in some measure disincarnate. Of course I had wanted his body but only in the sense that his body was an integral part of him.

Now my feelings for him were to take on an increasingly overwhelming sexual character. I wanted him urgently, frantically, and I was going to have him. On Friday I would go to his flat, sit opposite him in the grey leather armchair, talk to him and, by this very act, our union would be consummated. In my mind this social union would, by proxy as it were, be the accomplishment of the physical act.

I trembled internally with excitement. My virginity had been reconstituted. I was going to yield it to Luc.

By Friday my excitement had increased to a point of numbness.

As things turned out, the session was pedestrian; forty-five minutes of stopping and starting and getting nowhere. I expressed aggrieved resentment about having resumed therapy and gloomy prognostications about its future. He didn't seem to be on particularly good form. I left with my virginity intact.

My lover had proved to be impotent.

There followed a period during which the sessions revolved around two major items: my rage about the way he had abandoned me when I was in Africa and my increasingly obsessive desire for him.

These feelings were incompatible. They couldn't coexist. My mind was an emotional battlefield.

Now that we had talked about it, no longer could there be the faintest shred of doubt in my mind. He had received my letters; he had known that I wanted to communicate with him and come back to see him. I had to face the fact that he had simply ignored this. The fury I felt was inexpressible. It was doubly inexpressible in that it seemed that the only way I could fully express it was by rupturing my relationship with him. I wanted to be able to scream at him, 'You don't want me, you fucker! OK, so I don't want you!'

But I couldn't do this because I was indissolubly bonded to him.

So the relationship carried on, poisoned and polluted by my anger which, as it couldn't erupt with full volcanic force, leaked out and spilled over in the form of aggressive jibes, fits of temper, periods of sulking or depression, and persistent questioning about his motives.

'*Why* didn't you write to me?'

'I've already told you – there wasn't enough substance in what you said for me to make any reply to it.'

'That's not true. It was only three sentences but it spoke volumes. It communicated the very essence of my problem. Yes, in a way it said nothing, but only to someone who didn't want to think about what it was saying, to look for its meaning. You're a therapist, you're supposed to be able to interpret things. Why couldn't you interpret that, a message which was so simple, yet so full of meaning? It's as if I'd made you a present of my most intimate thoughts and you rejected it.'

He said nothing.

'You've done a psychoanalysis yourself. In that case how was it possible for you not to realise the importance of these letters for me? Couldn't you think back to what it was like for you to be in this kind of dependent relationship and understand how much I needed you? How could you toss off that remark, 'You can write to me', without knowing what implications it would have for me? Maybe it wasn't the same for you. Perhaps you didn't have such strong feelings, perhaps you weren't so dependent. Well, don't use your feelings as a yardstick for mine!' My voice rose to a hysterical pitch of frustrated fury. 'Do you have any idea, any conception, the faintest notion even, of how I felt, stuck out there in Africa, reaching out to you, longing for you, and getting nothing back, fuck-all, zilch, as if you were dead, or perhaps someone who had never existed, a figment of my fevered imagination?'

There wasn't really any answer he could make to this. He alternated between silence (that convenient refuge of psychotherapists) and variations on the theme of insufficient material on which to base a reply.

At the same time I desired him terribly. I thought back in disbelief to my first impression of him, the asexuality and the total absence of male characteristics which had struck me. Now he was sex incarnate. His physical presence dazzled me. I would look at him sitting opposite me, unable to believe that such masculine perfection could exist.

One day he was out when I arrived. I waited on the landing, standing outside the door. As he came in along the corridor I heard the concierge greeting him: *'Bon jour, monsieur.'* I was intrigued by the idea that the concierge could see him like that, every day, getting his mail, exchanging small talk and so on, and for her, he was no different from any other inhabitant of the building; just another man who came and went, a person of no consequence. Now and again, if I tried hard, I could catch just a glimpse of him through the concierge's eyes, and then, for an instant, he seemed very ordinary.

He obviously cared about his appearance, perhaps too much so. As with Marion, I was ill at ease with any physical evidence which threatened to destabilise the image of the person which I had constructed. There was a hint of the feminine in the effort he took to be elegant and soigné, and sometimes he was overly trendy. The shoulders of the loose brown jacket were perhaps just a shade too padded, the baggy charcoal-grey suit a bit precious in effect. On one occasion he wore a frightful lime-green suit, a sartorial solecism which crippled the entire session. Thankfully, I never saw it again.

Although probably resolutely a man of the 1990s in reality, to me he was reminiscent of the Parisian Left Bank social scene of the 1950s. I could imagine him, darkly brooding, intellectual and romantic, hanging around till dawn in smoke-filled piano bars, an intense and sensual figure, bordering on the decadent.

One morning he seemed a bit truculent. 'You're in a bad temper today,' I accused him.

'You're very perceptive. I'm not feeling well,' he answered gruffly.

I looked at him more closely and diagnosed a bad hangover. This didn't seem right. Drinking to excess was a patient's problem. Physician, heal thyself. Or if not, keep your symptoms out of the consulting room.

The wrangling continued. Whichever way I looked at it, there was no solution. I couldn't leave him and yet I couldn't develop my relationship with him along any therapeutic lines because, after the business of the unanswered letters, I didn't trust him. I discussed it, analysed it, dissected it from all angles and got nowhere. I was stuck.

One day as I repeated my anguished question for the umpteenth time he said, as if playing a trump card: 'I told you that you could write to me but I didn't say that I would reply.'

I was dumbfounded by his stupidity. Obviously, this might conceivably have been his position right from the beginning, but there was no point claiming so at this late stage. I exploded.

'But of course you could have said that to me several months ago when we talked about it for the first time. It would have been very plausible. It's too late now. You've obviously just thought of that as an excuse. If it had been the real reason you would have said it right at the beginning. Do you think I'm an idiot, or what? In a situation like this you've got two possibilities. Either you tell the truth or you say nothing at all. Tying yourself in knots with these absurd excuses that you're just making up as you go along is the one thing not to do.'

The floodgates of my rage had opened and I let rip. But it was an adult reaction and it was at a directly personal level that I attacked him, pouring scorn on him, confronting him with all the faults in his reasoning, sneering at his pathetic efforts to talk his way out of a situation which was indefensible, drowning him in contempt. I spoke as a client attacking a business person in his professional capacity and not as a patient expressing transferential rage.

The atmosphere was tense when I left and I sensed that he was feeling sore. I began to worry about this, thinking that perhaps I'd gone too far and done irreparable damage to the relationship which, in spite of everything, I wanted to continue. I told him so, trying to back-pedal a bit, the next time I saw him. An uneasy truce was established.

A few days later I arrived at his flat in a state of morbid depression. As I sat down with him I turned the chair so that I was facing the wall and began silently to cry.

'Are you sulking?' he asked.

'No,' I sobbed.

'Are you crying?'

'Yes.'

'Why?'

'Because you abandoned me.'

'And what does that remind you of.'

'Nothing.'

'What do you feel, then.'

(Silence for a while.)

'I feel completely crushed,' I admitted finally, in a snivelling heap.

Afterwards I realised that our relationship had been spiritually consummated during that session. It hadn't been the idealistic scenario which I had originally imagined for this. Rather, it was as if he had furtively crept up behind me as I lay in a beaten heap, quickly copulated and slipped off again.

I RARELY REFERRED to the matter again after that. My desire for him and the expression of it, now no longer held in check by the hurt and anger I'd felt, came out to occupy centre stage.

It was inconceivable to me that anyone else had ever experienced such intensity of emotion. In fact this was a source of pride to me, as if I had the greatest emotional capacity ever known, a candidate for the *Guinness Book of Records* in this domain. It was a present I could give him, the knowledge that he was the object of the greatest desire ever to exist.

At that time I was reading *Les Cahiers Secrets* by Anaïs Nin, in which she wrote of her relationship with Henry Miller. Early in the book I began to feel threatened. It was unthinkable, really, but I was beginning to harbour the suspicion that the feelings described in the book rivalled my own in intensity. I read on with a growing sense of outrage and indignation. It wasn't possible. My desire was absolute, and no one else could achieve that. I sought reassurance in the idea that Anaïs Nin was an author and practised in the art of expression, which somehow falsified the thing which was expressed. She was a wordsmith who, by virtue of her craft, could conjure up powerful images and singular emotional experiences which bore no relation to the paltry reality on which they were based. I clung to this piece of sophistry.

Shortly afterwards the film *Henry and June*, based on *Les Cahiers Secrets*, came out. I hurried to the cinema, fascinated and fearful. I wanted to see, on the screen, the physical expression of this voracious desire I felt for Luc. I wanted to watch their naked bodies doing what I wanted to do with him. And as I watched I would put myself into the body of the woman and feel what she was doing with the man. But it mustn't be quite up to the mark. I still wanted proof that there was a substantial margin between my feelings and hers.

The film turned out to be a travesty of my imaginings. Anaïs Nin was a doll-like figure who, I felt, could neither experience nor inspire the faintest sexual tremor. Henry Miller was coarse and vulgar; in bed he was surely rough, sweaty and smelly. The sex scenes were arid and expressionless, like a series of yoga exercises. I was so relieved. I had been deprived of my vicarious fornication but I clearly surpassed my rival. I told Luc about it: about the book, the film, everything, so glad of this concrete evidence which I could give him of my superlative desire.

This desire was such that the thought of any woman in his life, either present or past, was intolerable.

His private life was a mystery. There was virtually no sign of any social or domestic activity to be seen in the flat, no indication of a second presence. Very early on, before I had got to the stage where I would have been unable to bear hearing the answer to such a question, I had asked him, 'Are you married?'

'That's not a question which I would answer.'

Why not? I wondered. Given that he lived there, it would be very difficult to keep the matter secret. I decided that he couldn't be. Otherwise it would be obvious.

There was something of the playboy about him and his flat, I thought. Perhaps his sex life was a series of brief affairs. I scrutinised his face every time I saw him, looking for signs of fatigue, proof that he'd passed a night without much sleep, entwined in the naked body of a woman.

The bar in the sitting room became more menacing than ever. At first it had just been a horribly kitsch item of furniture but now it came to represent something. It constituted incontrovertible evidence that there were females in his life, or at least that he wanted to lure them into it. Those impractical stools were not sat upon while watching television, when having parents round for dinner or chatting about work with colleagues. Their only possible function was to provide the setting for a seduction scene.

I didn't dare look at that part of the room because of the images it conjured up – Luc and a woman sitting on the high stools at the bar, leaning on it, toying with cocktails, faces close. It was still horribly vulgar and tawdry, reminiscent of a brothel scene in a sleazy 1950s B-movie, but it was calculated to drive me insane with sexual jealousy. Even so, I couldn't reconcile him, as I imagined him to be, with the kind of woman who would be impressed by this situation. The only women I could envisage fitting into such a scene were cheap and gaudy – long legs ending in elongated stiletto heels draped over the bar stool, thighs bared, breasts spilling out, fluffy blond hair, hung about with trinkets, and crassly unintelligent. It wasn't possible. I thrust these ideas out of my mind and resolutely looked out of the window.

One day as I sat waiting I heard the front door open. Someone came in. My head spun round in the direction of the hall. I was trembling with fright. An old woman was there. She started to bustle around in the flat. The cleaning woman. I could breathe again but it had rattled me badly.

I needed him to tell me that there was no woman in his life.

'There's no woman here, is there?'

Silence.

'But tell me. Tell me there's no woman.'

'Why are you asking that question?'

'Because I need to know. I've got to know that there's no woman in your life. It's inconceivable for me that there could be a woman in your bed. There never has been. You've never had a woman, never had sex. You don't know what it's like. If I thought that you had ever fucked a woman, even once, I'd burst with rage, I'd tear you apart, I'd rip you to shreds. For me you're a virgin. You're mine, and you've never known any other woman.'

There was a certain incompatibility, though, between this notion and the fact that he was a seemingly normal person and that normal people have sex lives. I resolved this contradiction by persuading myself that he was homosexual. The more I thought about it the more feasible it seemed. The slight build, the over-attention to his physical appearance, the gentleness which was sometimes manifest in his character – all helped to reinforce this conviction.

'Are you homosexual?'

'Why do you think that?'

'Because it's the only solution for me. As far as I'm concerned it's impossible for you to have sexual relationships with women, so it's got to be with men.'

I still had a doubt, though. In fact, there were two distinct, and contradictory, systems of thought which coexisted in my mind. On the one hand, he was the chaste celibate whose only experience of women was the metaphorical sexual congress represented by his verbal intercourse with me. On the other, he was a normal hetero-sexual but, as a psychotherapist, he had to keep the details of his private life hidden from his patients, which was why there was no evidence of it in the flat. I didn't know at the time how big the flat was and assumed that there were several other rooms, out of sight, with perhaps a second door leading out to the service staircase by which women who spent the night with him could slip in and out unseen.

But I must never come across any trace of this heterosexual activity. It was as if the whole area around his flat was radioactive, a no-go area. I could no longer do my shopping in the market that I used to go to because it was so close to where he lived. I trembled at the thought of coming across him, accompanied by some female, in the boulangerie, queuing at the greengrocer's or poring over the frozen food counter in the supermarket. The cinema was also a source of danger. I would only go to films which I thought he would be unlikely to be interested in and in areas which I didn't expect him to frequent (a rather pointless set of precautions as I had no real criteria by which to gauge his inclinations in either of these respects).

All my mental and emotional energies were monopolised by the relationship. Since coming back to Paris I had arranged to work from home as this freed me from the need to function as a member of society on a daily basis. I worked in solitude, only when I felt able to, and with half my mind on Luc. Most of the time I was in a state of abstraction and had to make a conscious effort to concentrate on the present when I was interacting with other people. Sometimes my mind would be drawn away by the magnet of Luc and I would suddenly come back to reality to find that the person I was supposed to be talking to was looking a bit puzzled. It was embarrassing. How long had I been 'absent'? Had I just been asked a question? I had no idea.

I was somewhat reassured when, reading a book by a journalist who had spent ten years in analysis with Lacan, a famous French psychoanalyst, I found this same feeling of being 'elsewhere' described. Obviously it was a common symptom. I was less reassured to find him say that if Lacan had asked him to join him in the Antipodes for an interview of twenty seconds for a fee of ten million francs he would have found the money and gone. Again I felt threatened by the expression of a desire which perhaps rivalled my own in intensity. I explained it away, as with Anaïs Nin. The man was a journalist. A flourish of the pen and he turned out a piece of literary hyperbole.

But it still made me uneasy. I took the problem to Luc.

'I know that I desire you more than anyone has ever desired anyone else in the world, but here's this guy saying that he'd have gone to the ends of the earth to spend just twenty seconds with Lacan. It's preposterous to say such a thing. No one would ever do that, so his words are meaningless. They bear no relationship to reality, not even to his emotional reality. I have to admit that I wouldn't do that even for you, but that doesn't diminish my desire for you.'

'But you really did come from the other side of the world for me. You came back from Africa.'

This was true. I had used my holiday to visit him, six thousand miles away, instead of going to one of the many exotic places nearby. I was pleased that he had recognised that.

My abstracted state was due to the fact that I was living increasingly in a world of sexual fantasy, but fantasies of such clarity and intensity that the word 'fantasy' no longer seemed appropriate. Previously, sexual fantasies for me had meant thinking of a man whom I desired, imagining sexual scenarios with him and experiencing the corresponding physical urges, desires and satisfactions.

This was different. The simple thought of him, the person only, without any physical or sexual associations coming to mind, brought my body to a state of sexual arousal. The idea of being alone in that room with him, sitting opposite him, did likewise. I squirmed with pleasure, my chest was constricted, my limbs weak. He was between my legs.

The actual sexual reveries which he induced took me onto another plane. I discovered a whole new world of auto-eroticism which I had not known existed. A world of activity so varied and exciting that the actual physical presence of the man barely seemed necessary. In the end there was little that I could do with a man that I couldn't do myself, provided that the man, this man, was there in my head. And his presence in my head was so powerful that he was also there in my bed and in my body.

The most intense orgasms were spontaneous, purely spiritual. It was as if he came to take me of his own accord. I did nothing but lie back, with some unseen force spreading my legs apart. Then, through my mind alone, my body would be brought to a hitherto unknown pitch of incandescent convulsion.

I would spend hours, entire days sometimes, in bed with him. One of the most exciting things was that I was never satisfied. Until then, an orgasm had been a culmination, but a final one. I was drawn towards it, it was ultimately ineluctable, but I would try to resist as long as possible because it marked the end, like the kiss of the black widow spider. But with Luc, even after the most exquisite orgasm I would want him again five minutes later. It only stopped when I was so totally drained of emotional and physical energy that I could no longer continue.

These hallucinatory experiences were occurring with increasing frequency, often in the most unlikely places.

Walking along the boulevard Montparnasse one day, looking for a kiosk where I could buy a copy of *The Times*, I suddenly felt his body materialise, interacting with mine. I started to tingle. I throbbed and swelled, moistly ready for him. It was difficult to breathe. Soon I was going to start gasping. It was delicious. I loved it. But not here, not in the street. Where can we go? I saw the Dôme, the cafe on the corner. Faint with excitement, I turned into it, down the stairs, into the toilet, into his arms. We were alone now. I pulled up my skirt, pushed aside my underwear, hand urgently searching, legs apart. My vagina was full of Luc, thrusting, pulsating Luc. Orgasm crashed over me, excruciating and everlasting – annihilating me. Yes, Luc, that's what I want. Destroy me. Fuck me till I die. I leaned weakly against the wall.

Another time, browsing around the shelves in the library I started to feel it, like an itch. It irritated me at first. No, not now, I can't cope with it here; anyway I've got other things to do. But it wouldn't go away. It buzzed around in my body like a persistent bluebottle. Despite myself, against my will, I began to feel excited, terribly excited. Distressed too. There were other people in the library. They were sure to notice that my face was flushed, my breathing rapid and shallow. I stared at the rows of books, no longer knowing what I was looking for. All I wanted was to lie down, open my legs and be ravished.

And then it was as if the orgasm had begun. I could no longer hold back. I stumbled along, legs trembling, to the toilet. My body, groaning, rocked and shuddered for an eternity.

I had never been to the library toilet before. The building had recently been redecorated, painted from top to bottom, but the toilet walls were already covered with graffiti. There were a number of drawings of male sex organs, most of them badly executed and

38

ludicrous in design: a test-tube-like structure with droplets of sperm spraying out from the tip; an amorphous protuberance ribbed with veins like a contour map of some peninsula, and so on. But one of them (it struck me right away) was powerfully erotic, beautifully proportioned. It was Luc.

From then on, every time I went to the library I would go to the toilet to see Luc's penis. The place became for me a kind of shrine where I lasciviously admired, desired, lusted for, those very special genitalia. I didn't have to lust for long. I need only close my eyes and the penis would materialise in the flesh, my flesh, stroking, pushing, deeper, faster, wilder, bringing me to a pitch of screaming, fainting climax.

Later, this penis came alive in even more detail. One day, when the bedroom door was open, I saw his bed; it was covered in a variegated red and purple bedspread. In my mind the bedspread became associated with his body, as if I had seen him in bed, naked, his private parts exposed. The red and purple were the colours of his erect penis. I could now see it clearly, a reality which I had pieced together like a jigsaw puzzle: the sensuous lines of the drawing, engorged, bursting out from strong black pubic hairs.

He wasn't aware of any of this.

I began to talk to him about it, hesitantly skirting round the edges of the subject. I wasn't yet ready to go into detail.

'You don't have a woman because it's with me that you have sex. *Only* me.'

'You imagine yourself making love with me?'

'I don't use the expression "making love". It's got nothing to do with love. I fuck with you.'

This brought me up against a semantic difficulty which I had both in French and English. I couldn't use the word 'love' or any expression containing it. This posed a particular problem as regards sex as there was no expression which I felt comfortable with and I always radiated unease when talking about it, groping around with words which struck me as either mawkish, medical or obscene. Every time he spoke about 'making love' I would correct him and in the end I had him so well trained that he would invariably say 'fuck' in the same way as I did.

'Tell me about those fantasies that you have.'

'They're not fantasies. It's real.'

'What do you mean, "real"? You can't say to me, for example, "Hey, it was really good with you last night" because I wasn't there.'

'Yes, you are there.'

'Do you see me?'

'No, I don't see you but I feel you.'

'You feel me on your skin, in your body?'

'Yes. At least, I know that you aren't really there, but it's more than fantasy. It's as if I'd taken a drug. It's like being under the influence of LSD. The difference between ordinary sexual fantasies and what I experience with you is similar to the difference between normal sensorial perceptions and the kind of sensorial perceptions experienced when taking LSD. I don't know if you know what I mean?' I looked at him enquiringly. He nodded for me to carry on. 'For example, LSD transforms the experience of listening to a piece of music. The auditory and emotional aspects of the experience are enhanced and augmented, they take on other dimensions. It's difficult to explain. And, of course, what I'm saying is based on my own experience of LSD. It can be very different for other people.'

'Tell me about your experiences with LSD.'

'Well, I took it several times. Nothing extraordinary happened, no bad trips or anything. But I did have some rather strange experiences in which I regressed to being a very young child, and there were qualitative changes in things like sights and sounds, as if things were both distorted and intensified, made other-wordly somehow. That's how it is when I have sex with you.'

'We should talk about the content of these fantasies,' he said to me. I said nothing.

'Does it embarrass you to talk about your sexual desire for me?'

'No.'

It was true that in theory it didn't embarrass me. On the contrary, the idea of talking about sex to him excited me. If I couldn't actually do it with him, the next best thing would be for us to talk about it. But I was reticent.

'Are you afraid that it will excite me?' he asked.

'No.'

What a stupid question, I thought. If only I *could* excite him.

'Are you afraid of becoming excited yourself?'

'No.'

Of course I wasn't afraid of being excited. That was the state I was in most of the time and I was addicted to it. It was only later that I realised that the question he had just asked was approaching the truth. I wasn't afraid of becoming excited, exactly, but I was afraid of having an orgasm in his presence, one of those spontaneous orgasms which would just well up, invading my body in a series of shock-waves.

The couch seduced me with a character of its own. My eyes were continually drawn to it, as if to a devastatingly attractive man standing over in the corner of the room at a party. I was very aware of it, aware too of the fact that Luc had other patients who lay down on it. Sometimes the cushion at the head of it was dented and crumpled showing that a head had lain there recently. I desperately wanted to lie down on it too. The thought of doing so excited me terribly. It also frightened me. I felt that the sexual connotations of it were so strong that, against my will and no matter how hard I tried to suppress it, it would induce in me an orgasm. I imagined, with horrified embarrassment, my body stretched out on the couch, seized with sexual convulsions, my face contorted, as Luc looked on with detached and professional curiosity. At the same time it repelled me. To lie on it would be profoundly humiliating. I would lie there in virginal solitude, while the man I wanted to lie on it with would remain seated, impassive and sexually unmoved, behind me. Then I dismissed the whole idea impatiently. It was all nonsense, this business of lying down on a couch. What could be said lying down which couldn't equally well be said sitting up? It was just one of the items used in the domination game played by analysts. A couple of times he suggested that I should move on to it, subtly taking advantage of occasions on which I was avoiding his eyes to say that I might feel more at ease if I lay down. I recoiled like a prudish old maid to whom an improper proposal had been made.

I came to realise that the couch was an object of sexual stimulation and desire in itself, quite apart from its character as an item of furniture on which sexual activity can take place. And I think the reason for this was that I knew that it could be the vehicle which would transport me even deeper into this other strange universe which I now inhabited with Luc. I never spoke to Luc about this. It was too intimate.

He was appearing in my dreams now. I woke up one morning with just a fragment of a scene still in my memory: we were in his office and I put out my hand and touched his penis, fingers gently gliding over it in a single stroke, feeling, through his trousers, the hardness of his erection. I dwelt on this image for days, going over it again and again in my mind, lustfully milking it to the last drop of excitement. It seemed even more real than my waking reveries.

In another dream I was again in his office, lying on the couch which had transformed into a bed. He was sitting in his chair as usual. A number of unidentified women kept walking through the room. Strangely, this didn't disturb me. Then a child of about two came in and addressed Luc as 'papa'. I was devastated. If he was the child's father, that meant that he had had sex with a woman. I became hysterical. He reassured me, saying he didn't know why the child was calling him papa, and that children often said things which didn't have any basis in reality. I only half believed him.

I told Luc about this dream and how I'd felt. His interpretation was immediate and, I thought, unintelligent.

'That means that you want to have a child with me. You were in my bed, a child appeared. That means that you want me to be the father of your child.'

'No, idiot! How could it possibly mean that? If the dream was an expression of my desire to have a child by you, I would have been happy to see the kid, not distressed by it.'

He said nothing.

I stuck to my own interpretation. My need to believe him a virgin was imperative. But the birth of a child to him would be the ultimate threat, the incontestable proof that I was wrong. It had been a terrifying dream.

Apart from the ecstasy of my fantasised sexual activity with him, the relationship was usually more or less fraught. I was, of course frustrated by the fact that I only had him to myself for forty-five minutes, three times a week, whereas I wanted to be with him all the time. The scenario in which I imagined being with him was difficult to describe and to explain to him.

'You'd like to be my lover and live here with me,' he said.

But it wasn't that. I didn't imagine living in that flat. It wasn't my scene, and I was affronted at the idea that he could be suggesting that I would want to live in the presence of that dreadful bar. There was, in fact, no setting for my relationship with him. We were in another universe, a universe which had no dimensions, no physical characteristics. It was simply a void which we occupied together, in which we existed, communed and copulated.

During my sessions with him I was confronted with the fact that we were not in this other universe. Instead of being merged as one in some insubstantial ethereal region, we were therapist and patient operating in a situation strictly defined and limited in time and space. In reality my relationship with him could not be anything other than this.

I was unable to talk about what I really wanted or to describe these quasi-hallucinatory ideas. It was all so novel and unwonted and I didn't feel that there was yet a sufficient climate of confidence between us to allow me to venture into this unknown emotional territory.

Frustrated in my need to reveal my most profound feelings, I expressed anger and jealousy. From time to time I would still go into fits of rage about him not replying to my letters.

'You didn't care about me. You still don't care about me. You don't give a fuck about me and my problems. All you care about is filling up the spaces in your appointment book and the cash rolling into your bank account.'

Worse than this was the jealousy I felt in relation to his other clients. I imagined that, as with Dr Weissmann, they were all female, young, attractive, sexy and 'his type of woman', whatever that was.

'Do you still see Karen, the Danish woman? Does she turn you on? Men always fancy Scandinavian women. Do you have an erection when you're talking with her? And Nathalie that I met in the waiting room the other day when you were running late? I'm sure that's the sort of woman you like – submissive but quite attractive, looks like a secretary, the sort of woman you can impress.'

He would stare at me impassively as I got more and more worked up. Then I would stop each time as I reached a barrier beyond which words could no longer carry my feelings.

'I can't talk about this any more. It makes me too angry. If I go any further I'll get so angry I won't be able to control myself. I'll attack you. I'll wreck the place.' I spoke tightly, rigid with the effort of controlling my body to prevent it bursting out in a whirlwind of violence.

'Don't you trust me to prevent you harming either yourself or me?' His voice had overtones of saccharine self-confidence.

'How could you stop me?' I growled suspiciously.

'With words.'

'No, I don't trust you, and in any case I'm not a circus animal that you can control with a few words and the crack of a whip.'

'Perhaps violence is what you really want. Perhaps you'd like to attack me so that I'd be obliged to restrain you physically. Isn't this one of your fantasies?'

He was right. We'd already talked about my fondness for masochistic relationships with men, and the idea of being physically dominated by Luc excited me.

The difficult word 'love' cropped up again in our conversations. He would try to lead me into avowing that I loved him.

'Why won't you admit to the nature of your feelings for me? Do you love me?'

'No, of course I don't love you. I desire you. Love is an emotion which only exists in the relationship between parents and children and probably what differentiates it most from other feelings of affection is the extent to which it can be selfless and disinterested. In all other relationships the emotion, no matter how strong it is, is something else – liking, affection, fondness, a number of things, but it's not love. And when I say that I desire you, it's a purely selfish emotion, it just means that I *want* you, but I don't care about you. If something awful happened to you I wouldn't give a shit. In fact, I'd probably be glad. It would serve you right for not caring enough about me.'

During the course of one of these conversations in which I was confusedly howling with rage because he didn't care about me and instead lavished all his attention on his other clients, and at the same time vigorously protesting that all I wanted from him was the pleasure I got out of the sexual fantasies which he inspired in me, he quoted some words from Carmen:

'If you love me, I don't love you. But if I love you, watch out.'

'What do you mean?'

'Think about it.'

I did, and I knew that it applied to me. I was often attracted to men who weren't interested in me and pursued them relentlessly. If their feelings changed I lost interest.

I was now having to rethink my ideas and previous experiences of love, desire and other emotions. By this time I was wholly transported into the other universe in which I communed with Luc, a universe of which we were the sole inhabitants. My physical sexual activity continued as before. We copulated wildly at every opportunity, whenever I was free to lie down on my bed and let him take me, whenever he materialised beside me, tormenting me with his hands, his penis, so that I had to search for some hidden place where I could be alone and succumb to the inexorable orgasm. But in that other universe I was beginning to find that there was something more than sexual desire, something unidentifiable and ineffable.

It was some sort of pulsion or force of attraction, different from and stronger than sexual feeling, but with the same magnetic effect, which bound me to Luc. It was something which I kept on catching glimpses of, as it were, out of the corner of my eye. Then I would turn away again, deliberately. I felt more comfortable with the sexual desire. It was something familiar, and something which I could give expression to. This other feeling belonged to uncharted territory. I didn't know how to deal with it and it was far too intimate a thing to discuss with Luc with whom, in the real world, I still felt insecure and distrustful. It was as if I was standing on the edge of an emotional abyss, one which I hardly dared glance down into as yet, but which was indubitably the next stage in the process in which I was now engaged.

As well as this, I also felt as if I was getting into contact with some new source of energy. Despite the various negative aspects of my relationship with Luc, I found that the mental state I was in often invigorated me tremendously, flushing out the channels of my mind and filling me with an intoxicating force and potency. It made me think of the power which yogis call *kundalini*, a force which can be released in deep psychic states of meditation. *Kundalini* is said to control the deepest aspects of the personality, particularly the subconscious, and its awakening is one of the supreme yogic experiences.

Once, talking about my sexual feelings, I tentatively indicated that I had felt something else in relation to him.

'And what kind of feeling was that?' he asked.

I fled before the question, changing the subject in frantic haste. It was too early. Later on, once I'd established a better relationship with him, we'd be able to go into all that.

This was one of several indicators which suggested to me that the drawers of my subconscious were beginning to open, just a crack. I now felt that I was gaining access to emotional levels of which I had never known the existence. My whole emotional experience within the context of the relationship with Luc had taken on a kind of psychedelic quality. Another interesting factor was that the nature of my dreams was changing. They were vivid, striking happenings which seemed to surge out of submerged layers of my mind, directly relevant to my current psychological state and fuelling it with further material to work on.

Around this time, about two months after I'd returned to Paris, I had a dream which in retrospect seemed premonitory and full of significance. I had recently met a woman whom I had felt very drawn towards. In many ways she corresponded to my ideal person. I dreamt that this person was my mother. Her face was made of blue velvet. Then she died. The blue velvet face turned grey, crumbled, and disintegrated into a heap of ashes. Thinking about the dream the next day I was puzzled by the blue velvet face. I thought it might have something to do with the fact that my sitting room was furnished principally with velours and chenilles in varying shades of blue, though I really couldn't see any connection. Then I realised, with a startling clarity, that the blue velvet of the face was precisely the material covering Luc's couch. I say 'startling' because, despite the recent dreams I had been having, I had never had such a powerful sensation of receiving messages from my subconscious. It was like a supernatural experience. It was unnerving. Later, with hindsight, it seemed to me that it was heralding the death of something in my relationship with Luc. But how did I know that at this time?

ON THE WHOLE I kept to myself the activity going on in the deepest recesses of my mind. In my outward relationship with Luc I was increasingly acting with demanding, unreasonable, hysterical childishness. At this time my behaviour and manner of expression corresponded often to an age of about eight or nine.

The principal bone of contention was now his other patients. The idea that he should receive any woman other than me was intolerable. The presence of another patient in the waiting room paralysed communication. As soon as I heard the doorbell announcing the arrival of the person after me I would refuse to speak, spending the rest of the session in sulky silence. Feeling that this had no impact on him, I took things further. As soon as the following patient arrived I would get up and leave, even though I may still have had another fifteen or twenty minutes to go. I was enraged to see that this behaviour left him indifferent. He didn't care whether I came or went. So I decided to change tack. I wouldn't leave, I wouldn't sulk. We'd have a blazing row about it. I'd let rip and too bad if I got carried away. He'd assured me that he would always be in control of the situation, so that was his responsibility. In fact, it was a good thing that I felt so jealous of his other patients. It was the catalyst which would allow me to liberate so much of my negative energy.

I usually saw him at 9.30 a.m., his first appointment of the day. Often he wasn't ready when I arrived and I would see him flitting around in the hall, between the kitchen and the bedroom, as he had breakfast and finished dressing.

So it was on this occasion, the day for which I had scheduled the display of jealousy about his other patients. But, shortly after we had sat down, before I had even got round to talking about my principal obsession, I heard a sneeze just outside the door of the office. Footsteps tripped lightly across the hall, the main door was opened and someone left the flat.

My life stopped. It was as if I had had a cerebral arrest. I was brain dead. A deathly silence.

Finally, 'There's a woman here.' It wasn't a question, it was a statement. He said nothing.

'I'm going away.'

I got up and left the flat. My mind and body had fused together in a state of petrifaction. Downstairs, the lively Parisian streets had become frozen arctic wastes in which I wandered mechanically, like a puppet whose limbs were manipulated by strings from above. After some time the puppet strings propelled my feet back in the reverse direction, up the stairs and into Luc's flat. He looked as if he had been expecting me.

'I want to see someone else. Give me the name of another psychiatrist I can go to.'

'Tell me what you feel.'

'I can't come here any more. There's a woman here.'

'I think you should talk to me about it.'

'I've nothing to say to you. Give me someone else.'

'But if you have a problem with me, then it's with me that you should deal with it.'

'No. It's impossible. I want to see someone else.' My voice was adamant. For me the relationship was killed. It lay stone dead between us. He began to look unsure of himself.

'I'll have to think about it. I don't want to give you just anyone. I'll find someone before your next appointment on Friday.'

'I'm not coming on Friday.'

I sat in silence. When my time was up he showed me to the door. 'I'll see you on Friday,' he said.

I drank steadily all day. In mid-afternoon I phoned him, drunkenly pleading with him to give me the address of another therapist I could go to. He repeated that he needed time to find someone suitable but that he would do so by Friday. During the next few days I alternated between drunkenness and hangover. I didn't think. I just felt. I felt that I'd been psychologically beaten up to within an inch of my life. I lay in dazed, helpless, inebriated immobility.

On Friday I went back.

'Have you found me someone else?' I asked.

Despite having promised to do so, he started backtracking.

'I'd like to know first of all why you want to change to another therapist.'

'Because I can't stay with you. There's a woman here. I heard her. She had spent the night with you. Give me the name of another therapist.'

'But I think that the problem you have should be resolved with me and not with anyone else.'

'No. I can't come here any more, I've told you. It's not possible. I want to see someone else.' All I could do was beg repeatedly to be addressed to another therapist. It was the only conceivable means of salvation.

'I think that any other therapist will say the same thing to you – that the problem should be dealt with here, with me.'

I felt impotent. I knew, with a sense of utter infallibility, that there was no way I could continue a therapeutic relationship with Luc if I was to be exposed to the knowledge that there was a woman living with him in the flat. It rendered the thing impossible. There were about a hundred arguments I could muster to explain my position, all of which would probably be dismissed by a therapist as resistance. I could then produce an equal number of counter-arguments to illustrate the flaws in their reasoning. How many angels can dance on the end of a needle? So what? The critical fact was that I couldn't go on in the circumstances. The fuses had blown.

The conversation limped on. At no time did he admit that there had been a woman in the flat, vaguely implying that my assumption was based on a product of my imagination. This gave me a straw to clutch at. It had been a woman, of course. The timbre of the sneeze and the lightness of the step precluded it being a man. But it may have been the cleaning woman, that old woman I'd already seen in the flat, or a friend who was staying for a couple of nights, perhaps even the concierge who'd popped in for something. I clung to these hypotheses, not yet able to make the final break.

Finally, as a compromise, Luc gave me the address of a neuropsychiatrist, a Dr Paget, whom I could go to for a drug treatment, ostensibly to help me get over this particularly difficult patch, but really, I think, to give me the opportunity of talking about it to a third person. Like many doctors, Luc did not prescribe drugs to patients with whom he practised psychotherapy, preferring to keep the two roles separate, so this was a convenient arrangement for me.

I made an appointment with the neuropsychiatrist and went to see him a few days later. His consulting rooms were anonymous but elegant, with decor of a faintly Japanese flavour. Dr Paget was a nondescript but not unattractive man in middle age, with a firmness which belied an initial self-effacing image.

I explained why I had come to see him. He agreed that the

emotional state I was in warranted some sort of drug treatment. I then broached the subject of leaving Luc altogether.

'I've got to leave him. There's no good can come of it, so carrying on seeing him is just torturing myself needlessly. But I can't leave him without seeing someone else to help me get over it and to talk about it. I can't live with this dreadful thing bottled up inside me. I've got to talk it through with someone.'

'People often experience difficult periods in therapy you know. I don't think you should make any hasty decisions about this. It may just be a particularly painful incident that you're reliving, but you should be able to work through it by talking about it with Dr Landau, and the pills I'm giving you should make things easier.'

'Perhaps,' I said, though I didn't believe him. 'But if I decide that I really can't go on with Dr Landau, could you give me some kind of help for a bit to support me out of it?'.

He agreed to this, but said that I should carry on with Luc for a while at least to see if I could weather the storm.

I continued to see Luc three times a week. I was tense and disorientated. The things which had previously preoccupied me so compellingly were no longer of any importance. How could I still be jealous of his other patients when there was possibly someone with whom he had a relationship of infinitely greater intimacy?

About ten days later, again very early in the morning, I was nagging him about his indifference towards me. In mid-sentence I heard the toilet at the other side of the corridor being flushed. I heard footsteps crossing the hall and disappearing out through the main door. My voice tailed off. I sat staring at Luc.

'Yes?' he said.

I couldn't speak. The motor connections between my brain and my tongue had been severed. In any case, there were no coherent thoughts in my head, nothing which could be expressed in words. I continued to stare. Time passed.

'What's going on?' he asked.

I said nothing. I couldn't say anything. I wasn't able to speak. I didn't know how to.

'You don't want to say anything?'

Silence.

'Tell me what's going on in your head.'

My tongue was paralysed. My brain was paralysed. There was no communication between them. My body was paralysed. I couldn't move.

After about five more minutes he indicated that if I wasn't going to say anything then I might as well go. I didn't respond. He stood up, looking at me expectantly as if waiting for me to put on my coat. I didn't move.

He went behind his desk and sat down, fiddling with bits of

paper as if he was doing some kind of administrative work, glancing at me from time to time to see if I was about to get up. One small part of my mind was apart from all this, looking on. This part of my mind believed that he shouldn't be behaving like that. I was unable to speak, but I needed to be there. I felt as if I'd had a ferocious kick to the solar plexus of the mind and I needed just to be allowed to sit there till I got some sort of breath back. Anyway, I paid him for forty-five minutes so I was entitled to be there for that period whether I was speaking or not. I knew intuitively, without looking at my watch, when my time was up. Then I left.

Down in the street, walking on legs which wobbled unnaturally, I wondered if I was going to be able to speak to anyone else, or if I had been totally struck dumb with shock. To find out, I went into a chemist's and asked for a tube of toothpaste. The words came out, sounding strange, as if spoken by someone else, but it was my voice.

I thought about it all day. Without being able to identify the connection exactly, the situation reminded me of an incident which had occurred once when I had taken LSD. At one point I had asked a friend who was with me to give me a fright. I had suddenly had a desire to know what it would be like to experience fear under the influence of LSD. It didn't happen, in fact, as I immediately thought better of it and cancelled the request. But for some reason the noises in the corridor had the same effect on me. In the office with Luc, I was experiencing a quasi-psychedelic relationship with him. The woman in the hall induced a fright which in my hallucinogenic state I couldn't cope with.

The next day I was still unable to speak to him. I wrote out the LSD incident on a piece of paper and showed it to him. We conversed like that, with him asking questions and me writing down the answers. It was laborious and the content was of no particular interest. No parallel between the two events was ascertained.

At the next session I was able to talk again. I was nervous and wary, on edge, waiting for some sound from the other side of the door which would signal the presence of a third person in the flat. There was none. I no longer questioned him about it as the kind of sibylline response which I got was worse than being told the truth. Conversation was desultory.

At the end he told me he would be absent for five days and gave me an appointment for the following week.

In the meantime I decided that I would have to stop there. As yet I had no definite proof that there was a woman in his life or, even worse, living with him, but considering things realistically, it was obviously only a question of time before I would be confronted with such a situation. So, no matter how difficult it was, I had to get out now, while I could still minimise the emotional damage to myself. If I stayed I would not be able to avoid becoming witness to events and relationships in his life which I did not have the psychological resources to cope with. I had fallen into a trap in which I was exposed to too much reality. It was quite clear that the only situation in which I could have a therapeutic relationship was in the neutral environment and relative safety of private consulting rooms.

The following week I went for my session, emotionally prepared to make the break – a clear-cut rational decision which I would explain to him and then it would be over. It had been a profound and intriguing experience and now it had to come to an end. Of course I would suffer dreadfully but I thought I could do it because I knew that if I didn't, in the long run I would suffer much more atrociously.

I rang the doorbell and entered. Through the open bedroom door I saw an old woman, the same one as I had seen previously. She was dusting. She turned towards me.

'Do you have an appointment with Dr Landau?' she asked.

'Yes.' I knew right away he wasn't there. Something was wrong.

'I'm very sorry but he's not here today.' She smiled artlessly. 'I'm his grandmother. He's been held up because of the bad weather. He'll be back later this evening. Could you call him tomorrow morning to fix another appointment?'

Tomorrow morning, I thought, with a question mark. Tomorrow was Wednesday, and as far as I knew he always worked at the hospital on Wednesdays.

'Won't he be at the hospital tomorrow morning?' I asked.

'Oh, I don't know. I'll ask his girlfriend.' My ears thrust away the words. What were those distorted sounds I'd heard? There was some kind of mistake.

'*Who* are you going to ask?' I thundered.

The little old lady visibly quailed.

'A young lady who knows Luc very well,' she quavered.

I knew then, without a shadow of doubt. There was a woman who shared his bed.

I spent the rest of the day drinking. Emotionally I was stunned rather than in pain. Barriers around my mind stopped the evidence from crowding in. Gradually the alcohol created breaches in the barriers and the suffering began. I called his number just to hear his voice on the answering machine. Then I put on music which I played into the answering machine, over and over again: 'Parlez-moi d'amour', 'Je suis seule ce soir' and Nat King Cole. Much later I collapsed into drunken unconsciousness.

The next day I was unable to leave my bed. It was as if I now had two completely different states of mind. Lying in bed, curled up, warm, enclosed, I felt that I was in a state of survival, that I was coping, despite the monstrous event of the day before. When I got out of bed, for whatever reason, everything began to shake and tremble inside my head, ripples of fear lapped round about my feet, great waves of terror threatened to crash over me. So I no longer got up. I lay there for two days, only making an occasional quick, fraught dash to the toilet. Much later, when I was more able to consider things more objectively, it seemed to me that what had happened in the relationship with Luc was that I had been aborted, in a kind of reverse sense. I had been in the process of travelling back in time, going back into the womb. I was already there, and then I was brutally expelled, no longer allowed to regress in this manner, but now rendered so vulnerable, so dependent on the environment of the 'uterus', that I could no longer exist outside it. So my only remaining refuge was in the cocoon of my bed.

On the third day I got up. My psychological state had now taken on more familiar characteristics, although frightening in their intensity. Rage, outrage and desire for vengeance.

I had an appointment with Dr Paget that day and I intended to ask him if he would see me regularly for a while. I had liked him the first time I saw him and thought he might work very well as a methadone to wean me off the heroin of Luc. He had seemed sympathetic and understanding the first time I had spoken to him, and willing to help with drugs and a therapeutic ear. However, on this occasion he seemed rather taken aback by the force of my feelings.

'But this is sheer passion' he said with some bafflement after I'd described the state of hysterical anger I was in and given him details of my fantasies of standing down in the street and hurling boulders through Luc's bedroom window as he lay inside with the woman.

'Well yes, but that's what happens with transference isn't it. What do you expect me to feel in the circumstances?'

'Yes, but really, this is a bit extreme.'

He pressed me to go back to see Luc at least once more to tie things up neatly.

'Things can't finish with a broken appointment like that. In any case, you have to sort out this problem you have directly with him, otherwise you're just going to carry on lugging it around. You obviously have a problem of excessive dependence and it's been highlighted by this incident with Dr Landau. It has to be cleared up with him. If it isn't, you're going to have the same problems with me.'

As he said this, I sensed a wariness. He didn't want me to become obsessed with him. He was afraid of it. And in fact, although transference is more or less the linchpin of Freudian psychoanalytic practice, therapists often seem to find it difficult to cope with the more extreme manifestations of it.

I left with a prescription for antidepressants and tranquillisers; different ones this time as the first lot hadn't worked.

At this stage my feelings of rage and hate were still very much mitigated by emotional shock. I was able to phone Luc and tell him

I wouldn't be coming again though I didn't mention learning about the girlfriend. Talking about it would have made it seem even more real. Like Dr Paget, he suggested that we shouldn't stop abruptly in this way, without dotting the 'i's and crossing the 't's. I was non-committal and said that I would perhaps phone him after the Christmas holidays.

I then went to England, intending to stay for about three weeks. It was an ordeal. By that time I had become two completely separate people. There was the inner self which was completely absorbed in the relationship with Luc, obsessed with it, analysing it, trying to find solutions and explanations which would enable it to be something satisfying and fruitful, and at the same time suffering constantly because of it. And there was the outer self, the mask I put on when relating to other people, which talked and acted as if the matters under discussion, the things we were doing, were of consequence to me. It was becoming increasingly difficult to keep this mask in position.

I had arranged to stay with a friend I had known for twenty years. Despite our close friendship, she knew nothing about my experiences in therapy. I wondered how I would manage to keep things hidden from her.

I needn't have worried. Helen was so embroiled in problems of her own that she scarcely noticed mine, apart from commenting that I looked very drawn. I felt grateful to those people who were creating such havoc in her life, to her monstrous ex-husband, to her obnoxious ex-in-laws, to her taxing aged parents, to her quarrelsome siblings. They all took the spotlight off me. I let Helen talk. These problems were long-standing fixtures in her life and I had heard it all, or things very similar, before, so I was able to respond mechanically, my mind elsewhere. After about a week Helen began to run out of steam and I started to panic, fearing that some social output would be required from me. I was unable to provide any. Nor could I talk to Helen about what was going on in my life. She would find it embarrassing and incomprehensible. Worse still, she would think I was loopy.

I had to leave. I invented a rush job which Valerie had phoned me about, a very important piece of work for a major client which had to be attended to immediately. I fled back to France two days after Christmas.

I would phone Luc of course.

After countless hours of speculating and hypothesising I had constructed a scenario which I thought I might just about be able to live with. I attached a great deal of importance to the word 'girlfriend'. At least he wasn't married. This girlfriend that the old woman had mentioned was just a passing fancy, someone with whom he was having a brief affair. It might even be over by now.

After all, I'd always known with one part of my mind that he had sexual relationships. The important thing was that I mustn't have any evidence of it and above all, there must not be a woman with whom he was permanently involved, living with him. It was very unfortunate that these things had happened but I told myself that, in view of all the trauma it had triggered off in me, Luc would make sure that I was never exposed to anything similar again.

Luc had been away for a few weeks over Christmas. During that time I felt less pressurised by my feelings about him as I didn't know where he was. As I had no concrete circumstances in which to imagine him it was as if he didn't exist.

In the evening of the day on which I knew he was to return to Paris I was suddenly taken by storm. A tempest of rage seized me. I was battered and buffeted by a hurricane of fury. I knew where he was now. I'd seen his bed, with the red and purple bedspread. I could see him in it, naked, with the woman, twined around her, on top of her, his penis deep inside her, thrusting, gasping, screaming to a climax. My wrath was unbounded. It shook me and tossed me, it hammered around inside my head, for four days. Then, as suddenly as it had sprung up, it subsided, casting me down into a slough of listless, static depression.

I called him. 'I want to see you again.' We made an appointment.

We talked hesitantly, circuitously, skirting round the real issues. We arranged another appointment.

The next time I went we started where we had left off. I perched on the edge of the couch, agitated and suspicious.

'I don't know why I've come. There's no point in it.'

Luc was irritatingly silent.

'I mean, there's no good ...'

Water gushed noisily from the cistern in the toilet at the other side of the corridor.

Several things happened simultaneously. I left my chair, shot to the other side of the room, opened the door and crossed the corridor; Luc was behind me, one arm round my neck in a stranglehold, the other across my chest and lifting me off my feet; his voice was shouting, 'It's a patient'; a woman in her mid-fifties, dowdily dressed and utterly bewildered, appeared in the toilet doorway.

Luc carried me back into the office and threw me roughly down on the couch.

He sat down.

'You can't allow yourself to lose control like this.' He was out of breath and stressed.

'No, you're right,' I said, rather taken aback by what I'd done and anxious to agree with him, 'I shouldn't.'

I learned that the woman emerging from the toilet was the previous patient.

'I thought it was a woman who lives here with you. I was going to attack her.'

'Well, you see now that it's all projection, those ideas of yours,' he said, as if suggesting that it had now been proved that the things I believed about his personal situation had no basis in reality.

I grasped at this, using it to reinforce my conviction that there was no permanent female fixture in his life. I still hadn't told him about the old lady mentioning the existence of a girlfriend. Had I done so it would have introduced an element of reality which I couldn't face. Leaving it unsaid allowed us still to subscribe to the hypothesis of there being no woman.

I was shaken after the rather melodramatic turn of events. I sat where he'd put me down, at the top of the couch, just next to his chair. I'd never been so close to him before. My hand lay on the blue velvet bolster.

As I spoke about the terrible rage and violence that had seized me when I heard the toilet being flushed, he put out his hand and stroked mine. Later he took it and held it in both of his. I was surprised. And I was stimulated by it too; not quite sexually aroused (it was too innocent) but very aware of the physical contact. The act seemed to change the nature of the relationship, as if it was no longer purely professional on his part, but had an added personal dimension.

I was now subject to conflicting forces. There was the rage and jealousy about the 'girlfriend' which alternately ravaged me with violent frenzy or left me in a state of crushed and benumbed misery. But there was also the new intimacy of our own relationship. Even more than the caressing of my hand, I felt thrilled and excited by the memory of his arms around me in a vice-like grip, lifting me up and throwing me violently down on the couch, so reminiscent of a bed.

I was totally confused. My mind felt as if it had been dragged through a hedge backwards.

In addition to these new and conflicting emotions there was one major thing which had occurred and affected me with the force of a brutal *coitus interruptus*. All that rather mysterious activity of the subconscious, the micro-movement of the drawers, the sharply pellucid dreams, the quasi-psychedelic emotional and sexual experiences, had abruptly come to a halt. They had stopped at the moment I heard the sneeze in the hallway. This left me in a kind of psychical no-man's-land. I was no longer with Luc in that other universe, whose threshold we had just crossed, which I had just been about to plunge into and explore. But I had not returned to the real world either. He had abandoned me to stray around in an intermediate limbo. We had been involved in a fusional relationship and then ripped apart. He had been like an ineffectual adolescent, fumbling his way through his first sexual experience, groping ineptly, stabbing away with inexpert penis and, worst of all, pulling out just as he had brought me, albeit clumsily, to the verge of cataclysmic orgasm.

I had been seized with anxiety after the last session. Perhaps, when he thought it over, he would consider that I'd gone too far and refuse to see me any more. I wrote to him.

> I feel a bit better now. But I'm frantically worried because I think that perhaps you're going to reject me. And I'm still completely traumatised by what I've been through this last couple of months. It's as if my arms and legs had been amputated. I'm completely dependent on you. I can't live without you.

This was the terrifying thing. I really felt that I couldn't live without him, that I had been reduced to a state of total impotence, and yet I felt also that the relationship, as a therapeutic process, had been rendered completely sterile. Logically, it was absurd to worry about him rejecting me because there could be no positive outcome of continuing to see him. The paradox of the situation drove me even more crazy.

My activities in the real world had almost come to a halt. I was so perturbed by the experiences I was going through that it was virtually impossible for me to communicate socially. I reduced personal contact to the minimum. Even the few get-togethers or phone calls which I could not avoid were an intolerable strain as I struggled to act as if I was the same person as I had been several months previously.

I now worked for Valerie on an hourly basis and I arranged to do just enough to keep me ticking over financially. Even so, I was having to work at odd hours, taking advantage of those moments when I felt marginally better, rushing through as much as I could at that time because I never knew when a period of total incapacity would strike me. I was curiously remote with Valerie when we met or spoke on the phone. It distressed me to think that she must be aware that some alienating influence had crept between us but I couldn't broach the subject. There was no way I could make it comprehensible to her.

Mundane domestic activities took on the character of insurmountable obstacles. Cooking was out of the question. Once a week I would buy a cooked chicken, which was enough to last seven days. Apart from that I ate large quantities of peanuts and apples, plus a few other things like cheese which involved no effort and could easily be picked up by reaching out at random as I wandered abstractedly round the supermarket. Dirty dishes piled up in the kitchen until there were no clean ones left, at which point I would give them all a rapid and superficial wipe. Dust accumulated. Disorder increased. One morning I discovered that a pan of rice which I had put on the cooker fifteen hours before was slowly charring to a cinder. I had noticed a smell of burning the previous evening but had been too distracted to identify the source.

I was spending long periods of time in a state of absolute immobility, my mind vacant, staring unseeingly ahead of me. These states would occur without me even realising it, as if I had passed unknowingly into a kind of automatic pilot mode. Getting dressed in the morning could be a long drawn-out business. Finding clothes to put on was one of those practical activities which were almost beyond my ability to cope with. Then, often, half-dressed, I would come back to full consciousness and the realisation that I had just spent some indeterminate age gazing into space. During these absences from the real world I was roaming around in the limbo where I had been so cruelly cast off, suffering on account of my loss, but not able to identify what it was exactly that had been lost. But sometimes the absences were total, which was more alarming, such as the time I was in a supermarket and the next thing of which I was aware was of being in the metro. I had no recollection of the intervening period or of how I had got there.

I began to regret the note I had sent him as I felt it conveyed ideas which there was no point admitting to him. I hurriedly dashed off another one.

I'm only continuing to see you because I'm incapable of stopping. I don't believe that things can develop now as they ought to have done. It's just a horrible mess. But I can't face starting all over again with someone else. I'm welded to you. It would have had to end one day, of course, but in a natural way. Not now. It's too soon. It's like an abortion. Or it's as if I'd been taking a psychedelic drug with someone looking after me to make sure that things went well, and then that person suddenly abandoned me. I was involved in a process with you which couldn't be brutally interrupted like that without plunging me into a kind of madness.

These two similes seemed very apt. My state of hyper-vulnerability and total inability to do anything required by the process of living must, I thought, correspond to the condition of an embryo prematurely expelled from the womb. On the more psychic side, I was still to some extent in the state induced originally by my relationship with Luc, but in the sense that I remained cast off in some outer darkness, unable to find my way back into the real universe.

The next time I saw him after the toilet incident he was in a rather prim and starchy mood at first, making a comment to the effect that I ought to be grateful to him for continuing to receive me after my unacceptable behaviour.

'But what do you expect? How else could I react? Don't you

56

know how far you can push someone? Of course if I hear what I assume to be a woman in your flat it's going to drive me crazy.'

'My private life is none of your business.'

'Don't give me such fucking bullshit. It's completely unrealistic for a therapist to expect his patients to have transferential feelings about him, often extremely powerful ones, and at the same time to make a complete distinction between the professional person sitting opposite them in the consulting room and the person who has a personal life and an intimate personal relationship with someone who can be heard moving around at the other side of the consulting room door.'

He made no reply to this, instead changing tack.

'I've been thinking about your problem. Perhaps it'll be possible for me to see you at the hospital where I work. I don't know yet. I'll have to see about it and arrange to have an office. I'm not sure if I can. And I don't know if it would be a good thing for you to come to a psychiatric hospital.'

I snatched at this, the answer to all my problems. It was essential that he worked out some means of seeing me at the hospital; he simply *had* to get an office organised. I could no longer continue coming to see him in this menacing flat, with the imagined female presence lurking behind every closed door and the constant danger of coming across some item of female life carelessly left on view.

'Yes, yes,' I jabbered excitedly, 'I want to come to the hospital. I don't want to come here any more – I can't. Why shouldn't I go to a hospital to see a doctor. It's much better than going to his house. Only cowboys work at home.'

'I'll see. But in any case, I think I can protect you.'

I was saved! 'I think I can protect you,' he'd said. This was tantamount to him saying that he would never give me concrete knowledge of a woman in his life, that I would never see anything, hear anything or be led to suspect anything. We would always be alone together, without anyone coming to disturb our privacy and intimacy. We could carry on as before and I would resolutely ignore things which had already, by accident, been unfortunately brought to my attention. It wouldn't happen again.

Things did not turn out like that, though. However much I wanted to forget what had happened he was no longer mine, and available to me, in the way he had been before. At the same time I remained estranged from the real world, locked away in my alienated state of mind. Going to his flat was as stressful as ever. And finally, he was unable, after all, to make arrangements to see me at the hospital.

I was in agony. But there was a solution, a perfectly obvious and rational one. These feelings had nothing to do with Luc. They were the result of transference, so I would quite simply transfer them to someone else, someone who wouldn't flaunt his private life in front of me, someone older, with more experience, who would know how to go about things properly.

In some remote, intellectual part of my mind I knew this to be a feasible option. But it was a knowledge that held not the slightest sway over my emotions. That didn't matter, I thought. All I had to do was force myself to do what reason told me to do. Then, with the new and more propitious therapeutic circumstances, I would gradually be manoeuvred back into the mainstream of life. It should all be quite simple, really.

It was time for me to go back to Dr Paget to get another prescription. This time he agreed that it would definitely be better for me to drop Luc.

'He's supplied too many things for your imagination. You've been too exposed to his reality. But that's the problem with therapists who work at home, of course. It's the risk they take. The fact that you've seen his bed, for example ... well, really! Yes, what with one thing and another, a number of mistakes have been made.'

I was reassured by this. So often with therapists the patient has the impression that his opinions and reactions are only valid as indicators of his state of mind or symptoms of his neurosis, but this one was treating me as a normal human being.

'Your relationship with Dr Landau is anti-therapeutic,' he said, summing up. This comforted me as it told me that, no, I wasn't a wimp who was running away, scampering for cover at the first signs of difficulty. At the same time it was like a death knell. If I agreed with this – and I didn't see how I could disagree – it would obviously be absurdly foolish to carry on seeing him. But what if I couldn't break off?

As I had realised by this time that Dr Paget preferred to keep me at arm's length, I asked him if he could recommend anyone who could help me over the difficult period of rupture. He gave me the name of someone he thought might be appropriate, a Dr Hugot, and I immediately made an appointment.

When I went to see him I felt hopeless and dejected. I cried uncontrollably as I sat in the waiting room, so unaware of my surroundings that neither the dimensions nor the decor registered in my consciousness. A man of grandfatherly aspect came for me. He led me into his office. I carried on crying.

Dr Hugot told me that Dr Paget had already given him details of the situation. I took over from there, stumbling over the story, pouring out my feelings of rage, grief and desolation. He listened quietly, asking the occasional question.

'What about your previous psychiatrist, Dr Weissmann? Didn't you have the same problems with him?'

'Well, no, he didn't work at home. I knew he had a wife and

children but it didn't bother me because as far as I was concerned they didn't exist. It was as if the wife and children he mentioned were part of a fantasy life he imagined he had because, for me, he was a kind of troglodyte who never set foot outside that dreary office he worked in. To my mind he had no existence other than that. Of course I was jealous of his other patients and the people who phoned him but that was within the limits of what I could cope with.'

'I see. But don't you think that this business with your present psychiatrist may have something to do with your parents, something that you might have seen?'

'Perhaps you're right. I've no idea. Yes, I'm quite prepared to believe that a lot of emotional problems have their origin in some kind of infantile sexuality and early relationships with parents. But the point I'm making is that I'm never going to find out what the origin is with this guy because the therapeutic relationship has been completely wrecked. These things are very intense and delicate. I can see now why psychoanalysts need such years of study and experience, because if they put a foot wrong, the patient's had it. I've read of the importance in psychoanalysis of interpretations being made at just the right time. Too soon and the patient can't take it. An insurmountable resistance is set up and the whole thing is repressed again, perhaps even worse than before. That might be what happened with me. It was a situation that I was confronted with well before I was able to cope with it, and without having been in any way prepared for it, and it blew a fuse. In fact the whole power station went up in smoke.'

His face was expressionless. He said nothing. I didn't know if I'd managed to communicate anything to him or not. I carried on.

'But even apart from the actual incidents themselves, no matter how my reactions to them can be interpreted, they've made me realise that I can't have a relationship with a therapist who works in his own home. It's not a therapeutic environment for me. It deprives me of essential space. It just won't work. Don't you understand that?'

He stared at me unrelentingly.

'This space which I need and don't have with him – it's so difficult to define and justify. But I think it's similar to the psychological phenomenon whereby we feel uncomfortable when people come too close to us physically. There's a radius round about us which represents an area which other people – unless they have an intimate relationship with us – mustn't enter, otherwise we feel that our personal space is invaded. Well, that's the way it is with him. I need a certain space in which to conduct my relationship with him and I don't have it. I'm crowded out. And don't ask me to explain it or to look for reasons. That's just the way it is.'

His look remained impassive.

59

'This situation you describe is obviously of particular significance to your neurosis. I think that you have to sort out the problem with your present psychiatrist.'

He asked me for 280 francs and showed me to the door. He shook my hand and said, 'I remain at your disposal if you need any help.'

What for? I wondered.

THE BLOCKING OF this escape route meant that, for the moment at any rate, I was driven back into Luc's arms.

By this time I always felt very tense when I arrived at the flat. I would step gingerly over the threshold, looking around, ears pricked, trying to ascertain if there was any sign of the presence of anyone other than Luc and the previous patient.

My next visit was on a Saturday, at lunchtime; always a more dangerous period, I thought. I noticed on entering that the bedroom door was open, but all was quiet. I sat down just inside the sitting room and buried myself in a newspaper. A few minutes later the front door opened. I didn't react at first. After all, this had happened before – the time I saw the old woman come in. I slowly lowered the paper. As I did so I caught a glimpse of a young woman heading off in the direction of the bedroom.

The impact of what I had seen paralysed my mind which refused to register the images transmitted by my eyes. Above all, it refused to process the images into an incident loaded with significance. I'd imagined the whole thing, of course. Or a ghost had crossed the hallway. Yes, that's what it was. To confirm this I decided to go to the toilet, which would allow me to glance round and check out the rest of the flat. As I crossed the hall, I saw that the bedroom door, which had been open when I came in, was now closed. There could be no doubt: there was a woman in Luc's bedroom.

I slipped into the toilet and locked the door, locking out the scene at the other side. I hid, crouched down among a jumble of old magazines which lay scattered about the floor, squeezing myself flat against the wall. I felt numb, hot and cold, pins and needles, shaking all over. I had to get out of this place, flee, never come back again. I had to open the door and go before he came out of the office.

It was too late. I could hear him letting the previous client out. Walking like a zombie I came out of the toilet, returned to the sitting room to pick up my coat and bag which I had left strewn across the table, and went to the front door. He stood in front of me, barring the way. Without looking at him, unable to speak, I indicated, by waving my hand in the direction of the lock, that he should open the door. 'No, you can't go yet. You still have to pay me for the last couple of sessions,' he said, leading me into the office.

I sat down woodenly on a chair by the door, put my hand into my bag for my chequebook, and then stopped, immobile, staring unseeingly in front of me. He stood behind his desk looking, I think in retrospect, as if he knew what was going to happen. Suddenly, galvanised out of the trance I was in, I hurled the chequebook at him, scattering my bag and its contents all over the floor, flung myself across the room and threw myself at him, punching, kicking, screaming, hysterical.

'I want to go – let me go – I've got to leave – there's a woman in your bedroom – I saw a woman – she's in your bedroom – she's there now – I saw her ... ,' I gasped incoherently between screams and thumps.

He let this go on for a while (a few seconds? a minute? I didn't know) and then threw me down into his armchair, standing over me domineeringly, Rhett Butler-like, saying provocatively, 'Oh, but isn't she pretty, in a temper like that,' as I carried on snarling and trying to kick him. I hurled myself at him again. He pinioned my arms, holding me tight, and I screamed – a long, shrill, strident scream.

When the scream stopped he sat down, took me onto his knee and held me in his arms. For an instant I was outside of the scene looking on, a detached observer, in a situation similar to those near-death experiences related by people, subsequently reanimated, in which they feel themselves to be hovering above their own body, watching it being worked on by medical staff. It was such an extraordinary, unexpected thing to see myself lying in the arms of Luc.

I was then caught up in a kaleidoscopic sequence of emotions, all of which I expressed in a series of contradictory gestures; arms locked round his neck, hugging him, hands wrenching in fury at his hair, nails digging into him, head pressed against his shoulder, fists thumping him.

He took me firmly in his hands, holding me back from him.

'*Tu es jalouse,*' he said. We looked at each other. I said nothing, staring mutinously. I wasn't going to admit it.

'*Tu m'aimes ou tu me détestes?*' he asked. Again I didn't reply. I wasn't going to tell him how I felt about him. It was too humiliating. I could scream, tear him apart, wreck the place, but I wasn't going to say anything.

In any case, I couldn't say anything. As soon as this scene of emotional mayhem had broken out he had started to *tutoie* me. Despite the havoc reigning in my mind, I knew there was something not quite right about this. It was somehow false, as if we could (and yet I couldn't) forget, even briefly, that no matter what was happening it was still within the context of a professional relationship. I couldn't use *tu* with him, and yet I couldn't reply to his *tu* with a *vous*, as if I was a nineteenth-century domestic.

'*Pourquoi vous me tutoyez?*' I asked.

'*Parce que tu es un grand bébé.*'

It didn't solve the problem, but in the end, because I couldn't let it disrupt communication altogether, I continued talking using *vous*, but it was unnatural.

I loved being in his arms, on his knee, close to his face, touching his body, feeling his thighs under mine, running my fingers through his hair. It was a scenario which, although far from approaching my wildest dreams, was well beyond any which I had ever thought would actually be realised.

Paradoxically, it had been brought about by a situation which was still, to me, unthinkable. At that same moment, as I lay in a physical embrace with him, there was a woman in his bedroom, not ten yards away.

It was time to go. I didn't want to get up, to detach myself from him physically. I was afraid that when I did so the 'unthinkable' would invade my mind and force me to confront its reality.

We stood up.

'You'll feel better now,' he said. 'You're lucky that you're able to express your emotions like this. Lots of people feel as strongly as you do but they're not able to express it. And don't feel bad about it, about getting carried away like that. It's all right.'

I was surprised at his last remark. Bad (in the sense of guilty, which is what I supposed he meant) was the very last thing I was likely to feel. To my mind, even if I had blown up the whole building, him and the woman with it, it would not have been commensurate with the injury I considered he had done to me.

In comparison with the emotional hubbub and furore of the past hour I felt relatively little immediately afterwards, quite simply because I didn't know what to feel. I was in a state of utter confusion. My emotions were like the contents of a spin drier whirling round at top speed.

Throughout the day things gradually began to fall back into some kind of place. The most striking thing was that, although I'd felt a measure of relief as I expressed anger with Luc, I realised that it had been the merest superficial manifestation of my actual feelings, and so removed from them in intensity that, looking back on the afternoon's scene, it was almost as if I was watching myself acting in a play. The shouts, screams and punches bore little relation to the rage and fury pounding round my body in short-circuited passion. The slight satisfaction which I might otherwise have gained from it was further diminished by the knowledge that I hadn't hurt him. He had been able to parry even the most furious thumps and kicks in such a way that none of them struck home. It was just a game. But not quite a game. One thing had satisfied me, and that was the physical contact with him which, both at the time and in memory, I experienced as sexual pleasure.

The problem of the woman had to be dealt with. I had to know whether she lived there or whether it was just a passing fancy of some sort. There was no point asking Luc, of course. He wouldn't tell me.

I knew that he worked at a hospital every Wednesday, always staying overnight till Thursday morning. I would pass by his flat the following Wednesday evening and, if the rooms were lit up, I would know that the woman lived there.

I had to take things further than that. If the woman did, in fact, live there, I had to see her.

I worked out a plan and, as I did so, things seemed to resolve themselves. This whole business with Luc was largely based on fantasy; illusions which I wove around his character, rejecting those things which didn't correspond to the person I wanted him to be and magnifying those which did. So what I now needed was to be confronted with the total reality, meet the woman face-to-face, talk to her. The present situation in which I was being driven mad by muffled background sounds during the sessions, glimpses of wraith-like figures disappearing mysteriously behind closed doors, afraid to open my eyes in the flat in case I saw something I didn't want to know, was simply impossible.

So, on Wednesay evening, if there was someone in the flat, I would go up, ring the doorbell, see her and speak to her. Of course I had to have a pretext for doing so. I would hand over a letter. The content of the letter was no problem. If I found a woman there, it would be out of the question for me to carry on seeing Luc, no matter what the emotional consequences to myself would be. Much more than the jealousy and the multitude of other emotions that I was beginning to have in regard to his relationship with this woman, the one insurmountable obstacle was that my feelings for him were overwhelmingly sexual in nature and it would be absurd, preposterous, quite simply utterly impossible, to talk about these with him while the woman who shared his bed could be heard pottering about in the flat. I wrote a few words to the effect that I wouldn't be coming again and slipped them into an envelope.

The following Wednesday, after dark, I walked past the flat. It was about seven o'clock. There was no sign of life. I was excited and elated. Of course he lived alone. He was a confirmed bachelor, a playboy. That had always been evident. What did it matter if he had a string of girlfriends who stayed the night? The important thing was that there was no woman who lived with him, who shared his life, who would have children by him.

This last eventuality was, I realised, the most terrifying prospect of all: the idea that Luc could become a father, that not only a woman, but also a child, might one day live with him in that flat. The fearsome possibilities multiplied in my mind: catching sight of a pregnant woman in the flat, seeing a toy or some other item of baby gear lying in a corner. Worst of all, I was haunted by the idea that I could never be free now from the fear that during some future session I might hear the cry of a baby in an adjoining room and know that it was his. I felt that if that happened my heart would stop beating immediately and it would never start again. Luc must be nobody's father but mine.

I strolled on, sauntered round a couple of shops, then turned back again. As I passed his flat I looked up. The kitchen light was on.

There was a cafe just at the other side of the street. I went in and sat down at a table from where I could keep my eyes glued to the flat. The kitchen light didn't mean anything, I told myself. As he regularly spent the night at the hospital he had arranged a time switch for the kitchen light to go on and off. An obvious precaution to avoid being burgled. I took *The Times* out of my bag and turned to the crossword, but my eyes jerked back to the window. I chewed the end of a pen, bit my nails and stared up, eyes standing out like organ stops, as if communicating with a supernatural vision. A man sitting nearby began to give me uneasy looks.

About fifteen minutes later, after one of my rare glances down at the crossword, I looked up again and saw that the kitchen was in darkness. The five windows of the sitting room were now ablaze with light.

I wasn't really surprised. In fact, I was almost relieved as, after all, knowing is better than not knowing.

It was time to go and deliver the letter now. I walked round the block first. What I was about to do seemed like the greatest ordeal of my life. I had never had any clear idea in my mind of the kind of woman I expected Luc to be with, apart from vaguely imagining someone outgoing, intelligent, quite attractive and undoubtedly nice. Out of some kind of perversity I had dressed very badly for this encounter, looking shapeless and sexless in a pair of outmoded jeans and a baggy old anorak.

I forced my feet to climb the stair and forced my fingers to press the bell. A tall, thin, blonde opened the door. Her skinny thighs were tightly swathed in a mini-skirt, and she had a vacant expression on her face.

'Hello. I've got a letter for Dr Landau,' I said.

She took it with a limp movement of her thin wrist, without a word. There was no change in her facial expression. She closed the door. I hadn't heard her voice.

I felt arid as I walked away. It had all been much easier than I expected. I'd now shifted into another gear, one in which I couldn't even envisage going to see Luc again. How could I take seriously a man who had such a gormless girlfriend? I felt embarrassed for him. It was obviously one of those unequal relationships, not uncommon, in which an intelligent man pairs off with an intellectually limited but flashy woman. The dumb-blonde syndrome.

But there was suddenly a great, gaping hole in my life. All the emotional space which had been taken up by Luc was empty. It was as if I'd lost a vast amount of psychological ballast. My mind weaved about unsteadily in this unaccustomed state of imbalance. I tried to regain some equilibrium by drinking. I drank myself to sleep.

The next morning I felt crushingly depressed but this seemed a natural reaction. No matter how meaningless and useless I considered the relationship with Luc to have been, I was nevertheless experiencing a loss. But I would survive.

My next appointment with Luc had been scheduled for three o'-clock that afternoon. I spent the day working on a translation – a list of electrical specifications which required no thought as I knew them by heart. At three o'clock my hands ground to a halt, my fingers stayed motionless on the computer keyboard and I sat staring fixedly in front of me. I was like a character in some futuristic science-fiction scenario. Fifteen minutes later, like a remote-control-led robot, I got up, went to the phone and dialled his number.

'I want to hear you telling me that I can't come any more.' It was the first thing that came into my head when he answered the phone. I must have realised that the only way I could stop going to him would be for him to refuse to see me.

'But of course you can come. Why shouldn't you?'

I felt desperate. If he wasn't going to turn me away after what I'd done, going round to his flat at night to pry into his private life in his absence, what was I going to have to do to ensure that he would – wreck the place, turn arsonist, kick his balls off?

'You don't want me to. Tell me that you won't see me.'

'Of course I'll see you. My door is always open to you.' His voice was silkily treacherous as he took my hand and led me back on to the emotional trapdoor. I fell in.

We made an appointment for the next day.

I looked at him warily as we sat down. He was no longer the same person. Instead of being my therapist, my lover, my father, my mother, plus traces of other *dramatis personae* from my life, he was now, first and foremost, the man who lived with the dim-witted, churlish blonde.

And if the person had changed so fundamentally, my relationship with him necessarily had too.

I suddenly sprang at him, fists flying, feet flailing, screaming: 'Why are you living with that stupid bitch? – I can't see you any more – It's destroyed my relationship with you – How can you live with that dumb blonde? – It's demeaning – It's unworthy – It's grotesque – A tart – A bimbo – A moron.'

I stopped, out of breath, and lay back on the cushions of the couch, still trying weakly to kick him in the chest.

He fended me off. 'Wear high heels the next time. That way you can hurt me more,' he said coolly, grabbing my ankles.

There was silence for a while.

A butcher bellowed in the street below. *'Cuisses de dinde.'* The elongated French vowels hung comically in the air. Luc smiled. The silence continued and then he spoke. 'What kind of woman did you imagine me to be with?'

'I didn't really imagine anything. I mean, I didn't have a concrete idea, but I suppose, now that you ask, I would have expected you to be with someone like Anne Sinclair.' I was referring to a well-known French television interviewer. 'Yes, that's it, someone sophisticated, intelligent, attractive. But certainly not a bit of fluff like that. How can you?' My voice rose to a wail again.

'You're jealous.'

'No, I'm not jealous,' I hissed virulently, 'because one thing's for sure and that is that you don't fuck with her. That kind of body, it's fine when it's got clothes on it, but naked it's like a stick insect. Limbs like poles. It's purely for decoration, that kind of female, and it fits in with your flashy flat, but it's not fuckable. No, that's not why you keep her. She's just a kind of clothes horse, an additional item of decoration for your gaudy environment. Not only do you not fuck her, you don't even have conversations with her, because that kind of bimbo's got nothing between the ears. Now I know why you've kept her hidden all these months. It's because you're ashamed of her. You don't want your clients to know that you're shacked up with a floosie like that, your little bit of stuff. You bloody well ought to be ashamed, and now I know and I can't carry on a therapy with you any more because I can't take you seriously. All you care about is appearances. Flashy flat, flashy bird, flashy clothes. Arsehole!'

I tore into him again, fighting furiously, taunting him until I'd exhausted my supply of insults, even the wildest and most unlikely. I collapsed back on the couch. All the buttons of my blouse had come undone and it flopped open indecently.

It was time to go. He came and sat down beside me, speaking gently. 'You can't leave like that,' he said, taking the two sides of my blouse in his hands and rebuttoning it, slowly, seductively, as if he was, *au contraire*, undressing me. It aroused me and at the same time I felt wretched, impotent, done over and, in a way, raped – as if he was raping my mind and soul.

Now that I had unleashed to some extent the more irrationally based fury, I began to think about it more objectively. As I did so I felt a mixture of rage and puzzlement. As I understood it, he had tacitly agreed that I would not learn anything about his private life.

He had understood my fear of coming across a woman, realised that it seriously jeopardised any positive outcome of the therapy for me and undertaken to ensure that my appointments would be at times when the coast was clear. So how had it come about that the woman had come into the flat and gone into his bedroom in full view of me as I sat in the waiting room?

I tackled him about this the next time I saw him.

'When you said "I think I can protect you" you led me to believe that you would arrange things so that I only came at times when I wouldn't find anyone else in the flat. Was I right in thinking that you meant this?'

'I can't answer that question.'

'Perhaps it's a sentence that can have several meanings; which can be interpreted in different ways. So do you think that the meaning I gave it was the product of my own mind?'

He said nothing.

'But for heaven's sake, the purpose of a sentence is to communicate something – from you to me in this particular instance. And the words of this sentence weren't chosen at random. They were chosen in order to give the sentence its meaning. What was the meaning?'

'I can't answer that.'

It was maddeningly exasperating. I knew perfectly well that he could answer. He just didn't want to. He'd cocked things up and didn't want to admit it.

'OK, let's consider it from another point of view. The sentence "I think I can protect you" can have different meanings depending on the context. In this particular situation, if there hadn't been any other indications, it could have meant, for example, that you thought you could protect me from being attacked by another patient jealous of my relationship with you. But the context was much more precise than that. We were talking about my fear of coming across a woman in your flat and the measures we could take to avoid this situation. So, as the meaning of a sentence is normally related in some way to the dialogue of which it is part, it's natural for me to have interpreted it in the way I did, don't you think?'

The answer was again a prolonged silence.

The absurdity of this question and non-answer session increased my frustration to such a pitch that I started abusing him shrilly. A fuse was lit in my mind when he alluded suggestively to his sexual activities and I threw myself at him in a frenzy of aggression. He grabbed my hands to stop me thumping him, saying, 'You don't really want to hit me. What you really want is to put your arms round me.'

It didn't strike a chord with me. It didn't seem right.

'Why don't you tell me that you love me?' he asked, still holding my hands. 'Go on. Say it.'

'I don't!' I was almost gnashing my teeth with rage and the desire for revenge.

Outside of my sessions with him I was too weakened and debilitated to experience such emotions. That would have required an energy which I no longer possessed. My feeling of alienation from the real world was now extreme. It was as if I lived alone in that other universe to which I'd been taken by Luc. He'd left me there and slipped back on his own to the original universe to which I now had no access. I was stranded. My life was a chill, damp fog, interspersed with occasional incidents when, in spite of what was happening in my mind, I had to interact with someone or other (Valerie, the occasional friend with whom I was still in contact; a neighbour; a shopkeeper) and strive to give the impression that I inhabited the same universe as them. In other words, I had no life.

It was literally impossible for me to live without Luc.

I wrote to him after our last futile session:

My relationship with you is humiliating. It was already humiliating because I couldn't any longer accept the idea of an equal relationship with you after seeing the unequal relationship in which you're involved in your private life. It's even more humiliating when I realise that I'm imprisoned in a relationship in which thoughts and words are so devalued, so devoid of meaning and validity, that we would communicate more effectively if we just limited ourselves to uttering grunts and squeaks.

But of course there's no possibility of any kind of communication with you because, for you, relations with women are limited to the kind of primitive communication that you have with your bimbo.

And the most humiliating thing of all is that, in spite of what I've just said, I want to die because I can't exist without you. And I'm going to die with you. I'll come, during the night, and you'll find me in the morning, dead on the doorstep. If you won't live with me, fuck with me, give birth to me, take me into your mind, come into my body, then I can at least die with you.

And you're just a little wanker.

When I arrived for my next appointment Luc was on the phone in his office. I had to wait. I stepped just over the threshold into the sitting room and then turned my back, leaning against the table as there was no chair which I could sit on without penetrating further in. I could no longer face being exposed to any part of his environment for fear of what I might see.

As I stood there I thought, or imagined, that I could hear sounds in the kitchen. It was difficult to be sure as I was often tormented in this way by noises from other sources – the flat above, the stairway, the butcher downstairs. But the idea that the woman might just possibly be there shook me so much that I became rigid with terror, heart thumping, head swimming, nauseous.

Luc led me gently into the office by the arm and sat me down on the couch as tears started running down my cheeks.

'What's wrong?' he asked.

I said nothing.

'Is it because of what you wrote in that letter you sent to me?'

'I'm going to die,' I whispered.

'You're going to die for me?'

'No, it's not like that. It's because I can't get back into the real world. I was involved with you in a process which should have led to something, but it's not possible any more because you've abandoned me. It's as if I was in a spaceship which can't return to earth because something's gone wrong with it and now it's just going to drift off through space for eternity.' I wiped my eyes with the back of my hand.

'I'm not saying that it's your fault that I'm going to die. But for me you represent a kind of *coup de grâce*. My life isn't really worth living but things weren't bad enough for me to want to kill myself. This terrible, unbearable relationship I have with you will be the catalyst which drives me to it, and in the end it's best like that.' We sat in morbid silence for a bit and then I resumed.

'Also, it's the only intimate thing I can do with you. If I can't do all the other things I mentioned in my letter, I can still die with you. And even if it's only on your doorstep, it will be just a few metres away from you – in your arms in a way.'

He looked very serious. 'Rosie, it's intolerable to me to hear that sort of thing.'

'Well, in that case you shouldn't be a psychiatrist,' I snapped. 'Get another job.' The hypocrisy of his words had jerked me momentarily out of my melancholy.

Then I lapsed back into gloom.

I had had a strange psychedelic experience that morning. My imagination had run vividly through a scenario in which Luc and I were Siamese twins, with only one set of vital organs between us. We were being operated on to divide us into two separate individuals, but the vital organs were being left in his body. I was being discarded to wither and die.

I described it to Luc.

'But don't you see,' he said, 'if you carry out this plan to kill yourself that will be a way of killing me too, as one Siamese twin can't live without the other.'

There was something not quite right about this which stopped me short. I analysed it.

'No, that's wrong,' I shouted, exasperated. 'Now you're mixing up fantasy and reality. Killing myself is a possible course of action for me in the real world. Us being Siamese twins was a waking dream. And anyway, even if we stay for a minute within the dream, just for the sake of argument, I can see that it represents, in a way, the whole problem – the fact that I haven't been allowed to carry on in this joined-together relationship with you. I've been cut away. You're the one that's been left with the vital organs which enable you to go on living and I'm the one who's been abandoned to die. My death wouldn't make any difference to you. You'd still survive.'

He said nothing. Perhaps he took the point, but I had no way of knowing.

I changed the subject and started to talk about the terrible fear that was now ever-present, all-pervasive; the fear that the woman might be in the flat when I was there.

'Is that because it makes you feel guilty about being in my arms?'

'No, not at all, of course not. It's because she's deprived me of you in the sense that she's destroyed the image that I had of you. If you were the person I thought you were you wouldn't be with a woman like that. In a way I can understand wanting sex with someone you've nothing in common with. It can happen sometimes that you want someone for no obvious reason. Once I had a really torrid affair with a garage mechanic. He was vulgar and ignorant and a bit of a thug but, for me at any rate, he had a certain sex appeal, a certain style. There was never any communication between us. Just desire and sex.' I started to get very worked up. 'And that's the kind of relationship you've got with that bimbo,' I shouted. 'Only in my case I recognised it for what it was, just a passing fancy, and apart from that of no importance. You're so indiscriminating and brutish that you can't see this in your own relationship. With that piece of trash hanging around in your flat how do you expect your clients to trust you to show any sensitivity or understanding in your relationships with them?'

The phone rang. In any case, it was time to finish.

I left feeling much better after that outburst, but a few hours later realised that this relief was purely ephemeral. Expressing my feelings with Luc was a bit like having a cigarette, which relieves you of the craving to smoke for about half an hour, after which you start to need another one. By evening I felt just as bad as I'd done in the morning.

BOMBS RAINED DOWN on Baghdad, Scud missiles zipped over the Jordanian desert, Iraq was torn asunder. I lay sleepless night after night, with the radio on tuned to the BBC World Service. Every hour the absurdly jolly jangle of its newscast theme tune would herald the recital of more atrocities. I heard somewhere that the suicide rate had dropped dramatically since the beginning of the war, something to do with putting personal problems into proportion. I could believe this, but it had a different effect on me. It was as if the violence taking place in battle corresponded in some way with the emotional violence in my head – it was the vicarious expression of it.

I realised that if I wasn't going to end up in either an asylum or a coffin; I was going to have to look elsewhere for help.

Something I found particularly difficult was that it was impossible to discuss the situation with anyone other than therapists. As few people have (or at least, will admit to) experience of psychotherapy, it is difficult to elicit any empathy or understanding. In any case, even for people who have had therapy, the subject remains the ultimate taboo, much more intimate than sex, money or any other of the things which were once unmentionable. Bring up the subject of psychotherapy, in anything other than general terms, and most people will wince visibly and curdle like an oyster squirted with lemon juice.

I decided to put an advertisement in *Libération*, a leftish newspaper, in an attempt to make contact with people who had had negative experiences like my own.

On the day the advertisement appeared the phone rang early in the morning. My caller was a man who had done six months of analysis and then stopped because he considered it was doing him no good.

'How did you feel about the therapist during the time you were with her?'

'Oh, I suppose at times I felt quite dependent on her.'

'Didn't that make it difficult to give up?'

'No, no, not at all. I'd had enough. It wasn't getting anywhere.'

His answers weren't very explicit and his voice was reticent. It wasn't a very promising start. Making initial contact on the phone isn't particularly easy, and in any case the French are not very forthcoming generally about their inner lives.

It was his turn to ask questions.

'Are you married?'

'No, I'm on my own.'

'How old are you?'

'Forty-four.'

When he learned this he brought the conversation to an abrupt end. I suspected he had had another motive for calling and I was clearly too old for his liking.

Next on the line was Yvette, a dynamic, lively woman with a whole arsenal of home remedies which she was eager to propose to me.

'Oh no, you mustn't carry on with this nonsense, and you mustn't let it get you down like this. Psychotherapy is not the answer,' she cried blithely. 'It does much more harm than good. There are lots of other solutions, far more effective ones.'

As examples of these solutions she listed poetry, friendship, beauty and goodness-knows-what and invited me round to talk to her about it. I began to suspect that she might have something to sell, perhaps some sort of way-out Californian-type therapy; or perhaps she was the local rep for some Indian guru, or just a militant campaigner for the growth movement.

I discreetly enquired, with a few tentative questions, but it seemed that she had no particular axe to grind.

She overflowed with the desire to communicate. 'When can you come round? Can you come this afternoon? No? Well, any time you want, just call me and then come. I'd love to meet you and talk about it all. We'll sort all this out. Don't worry,' she said comfortingly, 'you'll see. There are so many things which can give pleasure in life, so much that makes it worth living. I'll be so pleased to see you. I've got a big flat in the 20th arrondissement; people coming and going all the time. You'll be so welcome.' Her voice was both cosy and energetic.

I arranged to go and see her the next day.

Prior to her call, my mind and body had been leaden with depression. Now I felt suffused with energy and the urge to rush round immediately to this generously maternal figure that had been projected over the phone and throw myself into her arms. She would make everything better.

A number of other people called, ranging from the outlandishly cranky to the most dispiritedly depressed. I was exhorted, in turn, to take up sophrology, to get myself a boyfriend, to think about people who had much worse problems than myself such as the handicapped, and to change to a macrobiotic diet. Only a few of them mentioned, rather cagily, the strong feelings they had experienced in relation to their therapists. It didn't seem to be a subject which they could talk about easily, as if it was touching the most intimate part of their being.

The following day I went to see Yvette.

From the images conjured up during our telephone conversation I was expecting to meet a large mother-earth-type figure, swathed in flowing floral clothes, clinking with jewellery, with masses of long, greying hair and living in a big, rambling, cosy flat.

The address she'd given me turned out to be a nondescript block of flats, modern but not very new, shrouded in an air of mediocrity. A thin, bony little woman waited for me in a doorway on the first floor. She took me into the sitting room and we sat down on black imitation leather armchairs, addressing each other stiffly across a teak coffee table. Four black plastic dining chairs stood with their backs to one wall. The opposite wall was lined by a teak sideboard, littered with china and glass ornaments, each one standing on a doily. A fluffy carpet covered the floor in whirls of black and dull yellow. A number of large, dark-green plants created an air of aspidistra-like gloom.

'Do you like orange juice?' she asked, pouring orangeade from a giant plastic bottle into two glasses which were already laid out on a tin tray on the coffee table.

We sat back, eyeing each other, glass in hand.

'So you had about ten people who called you in reply to your ad. What did they have to say?'

I summarised briefly and finished by saying that I hadn't encountered anyone who'd been through the same experience as myself, which is what I'd mainly been looking for.

'And what's happening with you and your therapist now?'

I gave a sketchy outline of the emotional trap I was in. I already knew that I had no desire to communicate with this person about anything of any importance.

Even from the little I told her she found the situation strange and excessive. She made a number of suggestions.

'Go out and get yourself a man, or several men even. Put your emotional energy into that instead.' She spoke as if she was very active in that area herself. I looked at the sexless little figure in the drab brown dress topped by an ill-fitting, bulky cardigan and found it difficult to imagine.

'Ask the therapist to have sex with you. The trouble's caused by all these fantasies that you're having. But if you actually go ahead and do it, then the problems will just vanish into thin air.'

'I don't think he'd agree to that. He seems to have a superiority complex about being a doctor and tends to be disparaging about therapists who don't have medical qualifications. He claims that they're the only ones who behave in an unprofessional way with their clients, so he's obviously not going to do so himself.'

'Don't you believe that, my girl. Kiss him. Try it, anyway, and see what happens.'

I was beginning to think that the woman was a crackpot.

'Psychiatrists are all stuck up and vain, and just as screwed up as their patients,' she continued, 'and a lot of therapists have sex with their patients whether they're doctors or not. I had sex with a female psychiatrist once.' She qualified this last remark by saying that she hadn't been involved in a professional relationship with the woman in question so I didn't know what point she wanted to make, unless it was to let me know that she was bisexual.

She asked if I was in the habit of taking the initiative with men. 'Do you kiss them or do you wait for them to kiss you?'

I said that it was probably the latter, or often simply simultaneous. She seemed to take a dim view of such pusillanimity, saying that she herself never hesitated.

Seeing that this radical advice wasn't making much impression on me she fell back into agony-aunt mode, asking me what my interests were and telling me to devote more time to them instead of wearing myself out with this fixation about a man who was of no significance.

Then she moved on to her own personal philosophy.

'I don't believe in God as such, but I'm a mystic. I believe in a kind of ideal and I turn towards this ideal. It's not God, and I don't even know if it exists, but it represents something for me. And even if it doesn't really exist, it doesn't matter, it's still an ideal. I try to reject everything which is negative in myself to leave an interior space for the positive. I'm drawn towards everything which is beautiful. That's the most important thing of all – beauty. That's what I try to create round about me. Physical beauty. Spiritual beauty. Emotional beauty.'

I looked around the ugly room, the hideous furniture, the oppressive cheerlessness of it all. It seemed at total variance with what I was hearing.

We chatted for some time longer, with decreasing enthusiasm, about various subjects in the interpersonal sphere: relations with men, having children and so on. I wondered how soon I could leave without appearing impolite. In a way I was curious about her. She seemed to comprise so many contradictions: her irredeemably social class D environment and appearance; her rather esoteric interests; the banality of her ideas, but nevertheless a certain eloquence and clarity of expression; the proclaimed rampant sexuality which seemed so at odds with the dessicated and neglected body. However, apart from a few uninteresting details, she was disinclined to talk about herself.

As I was leaving she sprang into life again.

'You must let me know how things work out with you and your therapist. Please do phone me and we'll talk about it again. Your story's so interesting. And if you want to meet any men, just let me know and I'll arrange to invite you round here with some people.'

We walked out into the hallway. 'May I kiss you?' she asked, a normal thing in France, meaning several pecks on the cheek. Taking silence for consent she leaned forward and pressed her lips against my mouth. I quickly backed out of the door.

WHILE STUDYING THE small ads in *Libération* I had come across one which, in view of the failure of my own, now seemed interesting – a group of therapists proposing an assortment of activities. I thought it might be some sort of centre offering various group therapies, where you could get together with people for whom therapy was an acceptable subject of conversation. I called the number. The woman who answered was uncommunicative but suggested I go and see her to discuss my needs in terms of what was available.

I went to see her a few days later. She introduced herself as a psychoanalyst, a claim which seemed somehow incongruous. I felt she would look less out of place behind a perfume counter in a department store than in this dimly lit consulting room, where she sat at the head of a traditional Freudian-type couch. Her figure was curved and voluptuous, moulded tightly by a black suit, the skirt of which ended well above the knee. Make-up had been lavishly applied and she was heavily impregnated with scent. Thick black hair flowed down over her shoulders. Her face radiated an artifical smile.

She spoke of the kind of group which she ran. There was one starting soon which I might be able to join, she said.

'What happens? How does it work?' I asked.

'Well, I usually work with groups of eight, and we meet once a week for a year.'

'And what do you do in the group?'

'Well, in my own case, I work with the image.'

'Really? Er, what do you mean by the image?' I was beginning to feel a bit doubtful.

'Dreams,' she said succinctly, as if this one word conveyed everything.

We discussed it a bit more, but I had already lost interest. A year was a long time, and I had never attached much importance to dreams, apart from those very significant ones I had had for a brief period with Luc. I tried to get some information about therapy centres in Paris but it seemed that there was nothing informal of the type found in Britain or the United States.

The question of Luc inevitably came up. I thought I might as well take advantage of being there to ask if there was anyone else she could recommend. So that there should be no misunderstanding, I specified that I wanted a man, aged at least forty-five and not working at home.

'This problem you have, you've got to sort it out with him. There's no point going to anyone else. Whoever you try, you're going to criticise them; you'll always find them wanting compared to the one you're with now.'

I trotted out all my usual arguments, with which I was now so familiar, and she finally gave me an address which I stuffed into my bag and subsequently lost. I couldn't really imagine myself going to a therapist who was an acquaintance of this improbable character.

Things were no better after this; in fact they got worse. I increasingly feared that if I didn't constantly knock myself out with alcohol or tranquillisers or sleeping pills, or rather a cocktail of all three, I would lose control – start screaming or talking to myself, or being really weird in some undefined way. It was as if I was insane with grief, but I didn't know what the grief was about. The feeling just banged around in my head like a poltergeist in an attic.

Crisis point was reached when I found myself in the middle of an urgent job for the agency, a catalogue for an art gallery which required particularly sensitive handling. I had spent hours with it, unable to convey either the essence or the style of the original. The panic induced by this, added to the existing torment, created a kind of vicious circle which brought the work to a complete standstill. It was a Saturday evening. I phoned Luc, writhing on the floor with anguish as I talked.

'I've got to go and see someone else. I can't cope. If I can't do this job then I can't do anything. I can't lead a normal life. I've got to have someone else to talk to but I don't know who. I don't know how to find anyone. I know you think that I should stay with you but it's not working. My life's not liveable. I've got to find someone else right now.'

The words tumbled out in my desperation to make him understand and make him do something.

'OK. If you really feel you need to go to someone else, then I suggest you go to the Institute of Psychoanalysis. There you can have an interview with someone who will put you in touch with an analyst appropriate to your particular needs.'

He gave me the address. I could hear loud music and the faint sound of voices in the background. He was entertaining, which may have accounted for the readiness with which he gave me the information. Previously he'd always discouraged me from looking elsewhere.

When I rang the Institute I was given an appointment for about a week later. During the intervening period I sank to what seemed like a point of no return. The doorstep scenario which I'd described in my last letter to Luc was seducing me more and more, like the serpent which hypnotises its prey. It was a scenario which would not only make possible, but totally transform an act which could not otherwise be countenanced. It would be the ultimate voluptuous experience, something both obscene and sensual at the same time – to die lying beside Luc. In any case, there was no alternative. Being alive, or at least being anything other than profoundly asleep, wasn't tolerable.

My mind was now wholly occupied with working out the details of how I could dispose of myself most efficiently. If I was going to die in Luc's building, I would only have a period of about five or six hours of night-time during which I could go there and make sure I was well and truly dead before people started emerging from their flats in the morning. I would have to go to the medical bookshops and root around in the pharmacology section to do a bit of research.

There seemed no point in keeping the appointment at the Institute of Psychoanalysis. In the end I went because it was near the medical bookshops, so I had to go to the area anyway, and also because of an excessive sense of obligation which forces me to stick to all commitments come hell or high water.

I sat in the waiting room with several other people who were obviously regulars. The general profile seemed to be young, middle class, intellectual. Each time a therapist appeared in the doorway to claim his patient I experienced a feeling of alienation, thinking that I could never enter into a therapeutic relationship with that particular person and wondering how the person he was leading off to the couch could do so. This triggered off a memory from my childhood. I was standing beside my mother in the kitchen, aged about three or four, and thoughts came into my head of my little friend along the road and her mother. As they did so, I felt a kind of pitying wonder. How could that other little girl feel good about her mother? This lovely feeling I had about my mother could surely only be inspired by her alone. Nobody else in the world could elicit such a thing. So how did other children manage without it?

My appointment was supposed to be at nine o'clock. Ten past, quarter past ... No one came for me and I began to hope that the dilemma of whether or not I should pursue this therapy business was going to be resolved for me, the appointment having been forgotten.

A few minutes later a woman came for me – sixtyish, elegant. I had no negative feelings about her, which was already an improvement on my reactions to the other analysts who had so far passed through the waiting room. She took me into a large, comfortable room. There were several armchairs, the inevitable couch, cushions. As we sat down, I started to cry, bitterly, wretchedly.

Then I stopped and, in a detached manner, told her how it had come about that I had made the appointment, talking at length about the relationship with Luc, how it began and how it had developed. At one point she asked me to tell her about my life prior to this. The question surprised me. I wondered how she could think that my previous life could be of any importance compared to the enormity of the emotional trauma I was currently experiencing with Luc. In any case, my mind seemed to have been completely emptied of anything unconnected with my feelings for him.

She persisted.

'Who are you?' The question sprang at me, sharp and peremptory; it brooked no evasion.

'I'm an outsider.' The answer popped out automatically, before it had even been consciously formulated.

I expanded on this, emphasising my need to live in a foreign country as it provides me with a plausible justification for the profound and irrational feeling of being a foreigner which I've always had in my own country and particularly with those who, by all objective criteria, I ought to feel most at home.

The woman radiated an intimidating competence; but I was too reassured by the competence to be overwhelmed by the intimidation.

'What do you expect from this interview? Why did you come?'

Faced with this person, the bookshop reason suddenly seemed frivolous and the excessive sense of obligation a bit hollow.

'A miracle,' I replied.

'What do you mean, a miracle?' This was obviously an inadequate answer.

'A solution to a problem which so far has been insoluble, the problem of being inextricably locked in a transferential relationship with a therapist with whom there's no possibility of identifying and resolving the conflicts giving rise to the transference.'

She had made little comment so far. Now she asked me if I had any questions I wanted to ask.

'Yes, there's something that particularly bothers me. I think he's experimenting with me. The fact that he encourages me to give physical expression to my feelings, bashing him and throwing things around, doesn't seem very orthodox. He says that the kind of therapy he's doing with me is psychodrama, but I have an uncomfortable feeling that he's just trying out ideas of his own and using me as a guinea pig. And even though I'm expressing aggression and affection and infantile sexuality I think I'm also expressing adult sexuality in the physical relationship. It's inevitable, I think, because even though I regress when I'm with him there's still a bit of me that remains adult.'

'Yes,' she replied, 'we mustn't forget that you have the body of a woman in all this.'

'And another thing, I've no confidence in him. I don't think he's any good, or at least I've no evidence to indicate that he is. But he just says that this is resistance. Everything negative a patient says about a therapist is put down to resistance, so you just can't win.'

'Well, no, there has to be a certain minimum amount of confidence if the relationship is to work,' she said.

Finally she told me that I ought to see someone else. Whether I wanted to leave Luc or decided to carry on with him, in view of the difficulties I was having I needed a third person to help me in either case. She would put me in touch with someone, she said, and asked if I had any kind of preferences.

'I think I need a man.'

'At the stage you're at it doesn't make any difference whether it's a man or a woman', she replied rather cryptically.

I hadn't dared look up at her very much. Throughout the interview I'd kept my eyes fixed on her feet, clad in a pair of pinkish-beige ankle boots which seemed the most elegant footwear I'd ever seen.

Nevertheless I felt profoundly shaken up by my conversation with her. For the rest of the day I was exhausted. It was as if she'd made me vomit, a kind of reverse peristalsis which brought up a lot of what I'd been forced to swallow, unable to digest, with Luc.

For the first time I could begin to envisage the possibility of leaving him. For the next few days I was relatively relaxed. The conversation had done me a great deal of good and I imagined that I would be passed on to someone who would be equally beneficial.

Luc

IN A GENERAL way I continued to feel better after my visit to the Institute of Psychoanalysis. But the one thing that consistently made me feel worse again was seeing Luc. Over the next month or so, the very fragile state of semi-equilibrium which I'd achieved after the talk with the woman at the Institute was completely destabilised by each of my sessions with Luc. In the few days between each appointment I would struggle to put myself together again, only to be smashed to pieces once more on the next occasion.

I told him about my experience at the Institute. He seemed relieved to learn that someone else was going to take me on board even though it didn't necessarily mean that he was going to get rid of me. Throughout that whole session I felt that he was really floundering. I thought to myself, he knows he's really cocked things up and he's no idea how to go about patching them together again. It was a terrifying thought for me. I realised that it was probably a matter of relative indifference to him – a case of 'you can't win them all'.

I was sitting at the top of the couch, just beside his chair. I leaned forward, with my elbow on his knee, staring right into his eyes, a few inches from his face.

'It's true, you know, that it was because of the talk I had at the Institute that I gave up the idea of killing myself, but now I'm disappointed about it. It might have been better if I'd just gone ahead. The *coup de grâce*, as I said before. But when I first came to see you, it wasn't to ask for a *coup de grâce*.'

The tone of the last sentence was both critical and interrogative. I expected him to say something. He didn't.

'Do you believe me when I tell you that I would have killed myself, that it was all settled?'

It seemed to me very important that he should believe this because it was, in fact, true.

'Yes, I believe you.'

I was struck by the strangeness of the situation, most of all by its terrible disparity which rendered it grotesquely absurd. We were conducting a professional relationship in a position of physical familiarity. We were talking about the crux of my being, whether or not I was to go on being, the chance factors affecting this and his place among these chance factors. To me this experience was almost the acme of intimacy. To him I was just the client between the one before and the one after, a name occupying a certain space in his appointment book. Yet I sensed that he was troubled. He did believe me and he was frightened. I felt he was really out of his depth. I wondered, not for the first time, how therapists can take on and live with the terrible responsibility of manipulating people's minds. But perhaps they don't consider that that is what they do.

After leaving him I felt that I was really on my last legs. It was as if I had fallen over a cliff and was still hanging on to some tufts of grass with my fingertips. But Luc was stamping on my hands to make me let go. It was a race against time. Would the woman from the Institute be able to send someone to the rescue before I went plunging over?

I anxiously awaited the letter which would put me in touch with another therapist. This ray of hope shone very brightly; I think this was because I imagined that the new person would, in some undefined way, be the exact equivalent of the woman I had already had such a positive experience with.

When it actually arrived I began to feel rather insecure; the person had now come into existence and I was afraid he was going to be just another shrink who would make no difference at all to the deadlock I was in.

This made me feel even more negative than usual when I went to see Luc later that same day. The negativity took the form of aggression. I was barely in the door before I started laying into him.

'D'you know what you look like? A monkey. All covered in hair, with your skinny little body and your simian features. D'you know the only thing about you that attracts that high-class tart that you're shacked up with? Your money. That sort of bimbo doesn't come free. It costs money. And that's how you managed to lure her into your bed. Because you're stinking rich. It's certainly not because of any pleasure she gets from having your tiny little monkey's cock poking her.'

The sound of the words I was saying served only to increase my anger rather than relieve it. Hearing myself talk about her being in his bed enraged me. I started kicking him.

'With all the money you've got you must have been able to buy yourself loads of women. It's not for your dirty little cock that they'd be running after you, anyway.'

I threw myself onto him with my head on his chest. I was punching him and hugging him at the same time. 'You don't want me. You only want me to come so that you can pocket your 300 francs every time. You need my money so that you can pay these tarts that you screw. And so you can buy all these gaudy objects that you create your garish environment with – your way of saying to everyone, "Look what a success I am. See how I've made it." You fucking pretentious little cunt!'

He stroked my head. I suddenly switched into observer mode. What he was doing felt wrong because it had no emotional value, or any other value for that matter. It didn't express the kind of feeling that such an act would normally be used to convey and, because I realised this, it didn't trigger off any reaction in me. Physical contact between us, for me, was sexual pleasure and nothing else because, despite what he kept on trying to tell me, I didn't love him: I was obsessed by him, bewitched by him, enslaved by him, but I didn't love him. And for him, it was just a series of hollow gestures which he imagined, wrongly, was serving some professional purpose. I liked it, I wanted it, but apart from the sexual thrill it gave me it was useless and meaningless.

'Why don't you let yourself go?' he asked.

'What do you mean?'

'You're afraid of your feelings for me. You're afraid to let me look after you like a little child.'

'But I don't want you to look after me like a little child,' I howled indignantly. 'I want you to fuck me, that's all. Even if it's only with your little monkey's cock.'

He started to laugh. He often did this and it always had the same disconcerting effect on me. I would suddenly join him in seeing the comical side of the thing and I would then be subject to a violent emotional lurch, like being in a dive-bomber at the fair, whereby I was flung from a state of murderous rage or frustrated exasperation to one of helpless laughter. It was very unsettling.

Before I left he asked me if I'd heard from the Institute of Psychoanalysis. I said no. The fact that I was lying to him was indicative of how much our relationship had deteriorated. I hardly ever lie. The fact that I had done so made me realise that I had no respect for him.

I made an appointment with the analyst the Institute had put me in touch with. In the meantime, I saw Luc once again.

We had one of our frequent arguments about whether or not the window was to be left open. He liked to leave it open to get rid of the thick cloud of cigarette smoke which filled the room. I preferred it to be closed because the street below was noisy and the room was often cold.

'Couldn't you close the window?'

'It's a bit warm, don't you think?'

There was silence for a few moments.

'You can take your jacket off.'

Even as I said it, I felt aroused. He smiled knowingly, as if he could see into my mind. He realised that I was really saying, 'Take your clothes off, everything. Let me see your body, your genitals – your penis, your testicles, your thick black, curling, pubic hair. I want to see them, to touch them, to put my face against them.' He saw all this running through my head. Or at least, I liked to think he did. It allowed me to feel that I was communicating to him something that I refused to put into words.

As I refused to put it into words I turned my thoughts to another matter that was preoccupying me, one that was almost as difficult to bring up. There were many things which I resisted discussing with him out of mistrust but sometimes the need to express something was so strong that I couldn't resist. So it was now.

'All I want is to get back into the real universe,' I burst out desperately. 'You took me into another universe and abandoned me there. It's like a parallel universe, everything's the same except that there's no means of communication between one and the other. And there's no way for me to get back. There are no bridges between one and the other.'

'Not even me?'

'Especially not you!'

I moved closer to him.

'I've something very important to tell you.'

I squirmed around for a bit, unwilling to acknowledge that he was someone to whom I could say anything of any importance. I forced myself to continue.

'Before (before what happened about the woman, I mean), our relationship was dynamic, and now it's static. It's like the way it was with Dr Weissmann. That means that it's never going to get anywhere, that it can't lead to any positive outcome, but all the same I'm tied to you, without being able to escape. With the other therapists I thought that it was very nice to have all these intoxicating feelings about them but I really didn't see how that could in any way help to sort out my psychological problems. With you, at the time when it still felt dynamic, it was different. I knew, without understanding how, that I was involved in some kind of process that would lead to fundamental changes in me. And it wasn't that I didn't suffer at that time – I've always suffered with you, but there was something *moving*. Now it's completely cocked up.'

I had my arms round his legs, pressing my breast against his knee.

'In the last letter I sent you from Africa I said that I had to come back, that it was as if I'd passed too close to a black hole and been captured by its gravity. It's a very appropriate metaphor and it still applies. Do you know, there's a certain point in the vicinity of a black hole where forces can counterbalance each other, and if you arrive at that point you're stuck; you stay there for all eternity. Well, it's like that with you. I can't make any progress, I can't resume being the way I was before. I'm stuck, and I'm going to go on being like this for ever.'

He looked very serious, as if he was concentrating hard. 'These are very complex ideas that you're expressing.'

I was irritated. 'What are you talking about? It's not complex at all. It's quite simple. You say that because you're stupid. For stupid people, even simple things appear complex.'

I abandoned the subject and hoped even more fervently than ever that the new therapist would enable me to break with Luc.

I went to see Dr Grosjean the next day. His flat was in one of those typically-Parisian, historic old buildings. I passed through a heavy wooden door, across a cobbled courtyard draped with ivy, up an uneven stone stairway and stopped on the second floor. The doorbell was answered by a man of about fifty, wiry and balding. He took me straight into his office, a large room furnished with the bare necessities: couch, desk and a couple of armchairs.

My impression, that first day, was of a no-nonsense man: sharp, direct and unpretentious. I gave him a rough outline of the story of my relationship with Luc and told him of my need to .find some solution to the desperately unsatisfactory situation.

His diagnosis was terse and to the point.

'There's too much confusion between the professional person and the private individual. You don't know what you're dealing with. And there also seems to be confusion about what you're actually doing with him. It's never been defined, the conditions have never been specified. You don't know what sort of context you're working in.'

All this seemed fair comment.

His next remarks were directed more specifically at my part in the drama.

'You must be able to see that it's projection, all these extreme feelings you have about him. There's no man in the world who's worthy of all that.'

'Yes, I do see,' I told him, 'but it doesn't make any difference to the way I feel and my inability to control it.'

A slight hint of impatience appeared in his manner.

'Well, the choice is yours. For you, this man represents the opportunity to plunge yourself into alcoholism, madness, death, to go freaking-out on human LSD. It's for you to choose if that's what you want.'

He finished by saying that, for the moment, this was a one-off session. 'I've given you a few things to think about. Go away and mull it over. If you want to see me again, phone me and we'll arrange another appointment.'

'And if I come for another appointment what will we do then? I mean ...' I wasn't quite sure what I meant but it wasn't clear what he was proposing in the long, or even short, term.

'If you come again we'll see where things are at then and decide on that basis.'

It sounded a reasonable suggestion. I felt quite positive afterwards. Although it didn't compare with the profound experience I'd had with the woman at the Institute, this man seemed to correspond with my needs. I believed that by using him as an outlet, a crutch and a sounding board I would be able to liberate myself from the terrible state of emotional bondage I was in with Luc.

Later in the day I began to feel a heaviness on me, something moving in me, exciting me. Those powerful, quasi-psychedelic sexual feelings that I hadn't had since before I discovered Luc's woman were stirring in me again. It was as if Luc, knowing he was about to lose, had suddenly become active again, luring me back to him, manipulating this sexual bond which chained me to him.

The next morning I went to the library. The graffiti was still on the toilet walls. I looked at Luc's penis, immediately aroused. I wanted to put my face up to the wall and lick it, run my tongue round the contours. I wanted it to emerge from the wall, become three dimensional, so that I could take it in my mouth, suck it and make him come. I couldn't envision, at any future point in my life, ever being free of these desires for him.

I carried on seeing Luc. I was still nowhere near the point where I could leave him. The situation would have to evolve radically before I could do that.

In an attempt to prove to him (and myself) that our relationship was moribund I told him the story of the dream in which a woman who had become my mother, and whose face was made of the blue velvet of his couch, had died.

'It seems to me that this was my subconscious telling me that my relationship with you was going to die. But I don't see how this could be so because it was prior to the events which have killed our relationship.'

'You believe in premonitory dreams?' he asked sceptically. 'I don't. I'm a rationalist.'

'Me too. I don't suppose it was premonitory in the sense of knowing something about the future that I couldn't possibly have known, but perhaps I was extrapolating on the basis of things which I had learnt subconsciously. I'm still puzzled, though.'

'Perhaps it was the realisation that there was something maternal in my relationship with you which constituted the obstacle. You didn't want to acknowledge that,' he suggested.

'No, of course not, that wouldn't be an obstacle. But in any case, for me the relationship couldn't include any maternal element because my desire for you is purely sexual.'

'You think that there's nothing sexual in the relationship with the mother. What about the Oedipus complex?'

'That only applies to boys.'

'And what about girls?'

'They want to have a sexual relationship with their fathers.'

'And how do they feel about their mothers?'

'They're afraid of alienating her because of these feelings they have about their father. So Freud said, anyway. But it's a load of old rubbish, that,' I shouted impatiently. Then I changed tone and started to whine, 'I don't feel well. I feel dizzy.' I'd been drinking very heavily the night before and was now suffering badly.

'Little children often feel dizzy,' he said suggestively.

'No, they don't,' I yelled. 'It isn't little children who feel dizzy, it's adults who drink too much. What a lot of crap you talk. And I see it coming. I always know in advance what sort of tripe you're going to come out with next.'

I put my arms on his knees, on his olive green corduroy trousers, and laid my head on them.

'I'm not well. I want you to look after me.'

'Like a mother should look after her child?'

'Fuck off!'

I was oscillating between rage and the desire to tell him about something that was making me suffer unbearably.

'I got drunk last night.'

'Yes?'

'I get drunk every night. And I take sleeping pills, tranquillisers – everything I can get my hands on – and it's your fault.'

'My fault? Why?'

'Because every night I've got to knock myself out, make myself unconscious. If I don't, I know where you are, I can visualise it. I've seen your bedroom and your bed and I can see you screwing that woman. And even if you're not actually doing it at any particular moment I know that you might be, or that perhaps you've just finished or are just about to start. So I've got to drink myself into a stupor because I won't let myself stay conscious while this is happening,' I shrieked in a paroxysm of fury.

I hurled myself on top of him, punching him. He put his arms round me to take me onto his knee. His hand slid under my right hip, cradling it, the tips of his fingers pressing up against the entrance to the vagina as he pulled me into a comfortable position. It was like a sexual caress. I was excited and at the same time surprised. Did he do it deliberately, one of his techniques to try and trigger off a reaction on my part? Or was it just an accident? It occurred to me that he handled my body the way an adult handles a baby. With babies it doesn't matter where you put your hands, but I wasn't a baby. I was an adult.

I put my arms round his neck, my head on his shoulder. Then I lay back in his arms like a baby. I wanted to be a baby, his baby.

I sat up again and as we continued talking I looked very closely into his face. At such close range I could see all his physical defects. He wasn't really attractive at all, and looked older than I had previously thought: not a very good skin, open pores, a narrow forehead with a spot in the middle of it, shaggy black eyebrows meeting untidily in the middle. Lines were beginning to deepen down the side of his mouth and he had a number of grey hairs. His breath smelled of smoke.

'Are you usually very jealous in your relationships with men?' he asked.

'No, and this is something I don't understand at all. Normally I'm not at all jealous. I've often had relationships with men who were

married or had some other woman in their lives. I just regard it as
none of my business. I've never really minded.'

'I think you did. You minded very much and you're taking it out
on me now.'

'That's not true!'

It really wasn't true. I had only ever been jealous of my lovers'
daughters, not of their sexual partners. But in the heat of the moment with Luc it didn't occur to me to tell him.

THE FEELING OF being stranded in a parallel universe was predominating strongly, and I was now experiencing it as a purely mental
condition having no connection that I was consciously aware of with
my emotional state. Communicating with other people involved
making sorties back into the real universe – a difficult exercise. I
vaguely remembered a science-fiction film called *The Bodysnatchers* in
which beings came from another planet and took over the bodies of
people on earth. This provided me with a kind of fantasy whereby,
each time I went back into the real world, I imagined my body was
being taken over by a bodysnatcher who knew how to play the role
required of it. Sometimes I had the weird feeling that I was observing myself, or the bodysnatcher rather, from outside. It was something to be managed, like a character in a play, to be brought on
and taken off as required. I would feel totally impotent, unable to
do the simplest things like operating the washing machine or making a cup of coffee. Then the bodysnatcher took over and things got
done, or at least the minimum necessary for survival.

Often I felt like a tetraplegic, utterly helpless, and totally dependent
but with no one to be dependent on – a state which induced panic. My
'self' seemed to be continually hovering on the brink of disintegration;
a slight nudge and it would shatter into myriad pieces.

I was in a prison of the mind, one from which I would never be set
free because there was no exit. I was alone there. Luc wasn't with me,
only thoughts of him. I was stuck there with my thoughts revolving
exclusively around my relationship with him. And as my relationship
with him was completely static, my thoughts just kept running repeatedly round the same circuit; nothing new, no development, no further
forward. Sometimes I got bored to death with it because there was
simply nothing in this other universe but thoughts of Luc. There was
no distraction for me, no alternative to this boredom. I would have
liked to have been able to read, watch television, listen to the radio,
but every time I tried my thoughts veered straight off back into the
other universe.

'You give me a great deal of power,' he said once, when I spoke
of these things. But it wasn't him who held the power. It was the
situation.

As all my willpower, or at least what little was left of it, was geared towards breaking out of this prison, I started to examine the emotional problems I was going to have to face in leaving Luc.

I felt it was going to be the supreme bereavement. Although I didn't love him as he claimed, I was sure I was going to experience it as the most devastating emotional loss – the most hard-hitting, shocking psychological impact I'd ever been subjected to. The sense of grief would be immeasurably more intense than what I had felt when my parents died, a realisation which distressed me as it made me feel guilty in respect to them. I wondered why this should be so. I decided it was probably because when you are an adult your parents are no longer the focus of your emotional existence, nor are you dependent on them. In any case, it is natural for the previous generation to die when they get old. It is something for which we are psychologically prepared in some measure. But surely I, an adult, could prepare myself psychologically for losing a therapist who was doing me nothing but harm? As yet I couldn't.

And because I couldn't, I carried on going to see him three times a week, insulting him, kicking him, punching him, torturing myself, frustration and impotence driving me crazy.

I nagged endlessly about the woman in his life.

'It's unhealthy the way you carry on, with all these games of hide and seek. Why make such a big secret about what's just a perfectly normal domestic life. You tie yourself in knots trying to hide all trace of that person. Of course if something is hidden people want to know what it's all about. It's enough to drive people insane even if they're not crazy already. How come there's never any of her clothes lying around? I only ever see yours. A bimbo like that's got only one thing in her head and that's clothes. It must cost you a fortune keeping her in clothes.'

'You're completely wrong in all the things you say about her.'

I didn't want him to say this. I felt that I needed to believe all the things I said about her. Either he should be trying to explore this need or he should just shut up, I thought.

As I was leaving that day I passed the woman as she came up the stair. She looked very ordinary, quite different from the previous time I'd seen her. Had she arrived ten seconds earlier she would have been coming in the door just as Luc opened it to let me out. All three of us would have been face to face – a nightmare scenario. It threw me completely off-balance. As soon as I got home I started sluicing wine down my throat.

Shortly after that I ran into one of his other patients. She came in just after me, while I was waiting. The main part of the sitting room had now been screened off and we sat facing each other on hard chairs in the dining area. I eyed her warily, poised on the brink of a hysterical fit of jealousy. She was in her twenties, amorphously fat with folds of flesh bulging out over a pair of ill-fitting trousers, a round, spotty face and a mess of untidy hair. I didn't feel threatened. She puffed at a cigarette.

'What time is your appointment?' she asked, glancing rancorously at me.

'Three o'clock.'

'So is mine.' She took a deep drag and retreated into her thoughts. There had obviously been a mistake and Luc was going to have to choose between us. Would one be sent away, I wondered furiously, or would we have twenty-two-and-a-half minutes each; if so, which one would be taken first, and what would that mean?

Luc appeared in the doorway. 'Suzanne,' he said and took her through to the office. Then he came back. 'Your appointment is at four-thirty,' he said, and showed me to the door, firmly putting a stop to my attempted squabbling about whose fault the mistake was.

When I came back I used the incident as a spurious source of resentment and jealousy.

'Did you have a good fuck with fat Suzanne?'

Silence.

'Is that why the cushions on the couch are all over the place? Because you've been fucking on it?'

Silence.

'She makes you have an erection, at least?'

'You want to know if my patients make me have an erection. You want to know if you make me have an erection.'

'No, not me, just the others. But you did fuck with fat Suzanne? It must have made a change from your stick insect, anyway. A bit of flesh for a change. Did Suzanne get on top of you? She must have crushed you. At least I'm smaller than you. There can't be many women who're smaller than you. That's a disadvantage when you want to pick someone up. That woman you've got is bigger than you. You must look ridiculous together. And what about the length of your cock? Is it in proportion to the rest of you? How many centimetres is it when it's erect? Barely ten, I should think. And what do you do with it. You've no idea how to go about fucking. You just get on top, bang, bang, bang, three times, and it's finished. Not like me. I do everything.'

'What do you mean, everything?'

'You wouldn't know. But I do everything with you. You can't even begin to imagine. Do you have an erection now? What are you doing with your hand in your pocket like that. Are you wanking? Do you want me to do it for you? Why do you wear these trousers in that thick corduroy material? Is it so that your clients won't see when you have an erection? I don't see anything happening there. Why don't you have an erection now?'

'You need to reassure yourself that I don't have an erection because you're afraid of the male penis.'

'What a load of fucking rubbish! How can you say such a thing?
If I was afraid of the male penis how could I have had the very
active and satisfactory sex life that I've had. What on earth are you
talking about?' My voice squawked with amazement.

Silence.

Afterwards I thought a lot about that last statement of his. I
examined it from all angles and couldn't find the slightest justification for it. Not only that, it sounded like a parody of some pseudo-
Freudian absurdity. I felt I needed to talk to him about it, to tell
him about all the ways in which my confidence in him as a professional person was being eroded.

As I sat waiting for my next appointment I ran through in my mind
all the things which rendered his thinking dubious. He tossed off so
many casual remarks which didn't stand up to close scrutiny. Perhaps
that was why the really orthodox Freudian analysts said virtually nothing to their patients. Every word in the therapeutic situation is loaded
with such meaning, open to so much interpretation, that it's probably
better to say as little as possible. Luc, however, could be quite verbose,
creating ample opportunities for pitfalls.

Despite the pragmatic approach I was now trying to adopt I still
felt as emotionally vulnerable as ever. While I was waiting I threw a
surreptitious, fearful glance round the room, afraid of what I might
see, yet anxious to reassure myself that there was nothing new to be
discovered.

Suddenly I saw that there was. There was a chess set on the
table. I couldn't bear to look at it. It was as if I'd seen his bed
again. I now had yet more evidence of his intimate activity with
others. Chess had always been an integral part of my relationships
with men, an extension of sexual activity. It was intolerable to think
of Luc playing chess with anyone other than me. At the same time,
I knew that if I could play with him I'd wipe the floor with him. I
didn't know whether that made it worse or better.

I jerked my head round to avoid looking at it and my eyes fell on
a magazine lying on the floor. It lay open at a full page advertisement showing a man cradling a baby in his arms. The face was bent
low over the child; only the top of the head could be seen. It was
Luc. It wasn't really Luc, of course. The chest was too broad, the
shoulders too massive, and anyway it was only an advertisement.
But it represented Luc. That was what he wanted to be: the father
of a child. That was why he had been looking at that page. And the
child he fathered wouldn't be me. I hated him for it. I hated him for
not fathering me and I hated him for leaving that picture on the
floor to taunt me.

As I turned away I saw that a new painting had been put up, one
of his. A child of about four or five, a small, dark, eager little boy,
dressed in a clown's outfit and framed in a doorway. The child was

what Luc must have looked like at that age. Painting it must have been a kind of wish-fulfilment for him, the expression of his wish to have a child, the child which wouldn't be me. I couldn't allow myself to think about it. If I let myself dwell on that I would simply go up in smoke and all Luc would find when he came to get me would be a heap of burnt-out cinders like the leftovers from a firework display.

I sat with my head cast down, like a nun observing custody of the eyes. There was nowhere I could look in that room without seeing something which shook me to the core. And it wasn't only items suggestive of relationships which disturbed me. I hated being in that flat because everything about it screeched success, not only material and social success but a kind of emotional well-being, which served only to exacerbate my own feelings of failure. He clearly had pots of money, whereas I struggled to survive. He obviously had an action-packed, and therefore socially active, life. The flat was littered with evidence of this. There was a white piano which was always open, with sheets of jazz music propped up on it. In a corner lay a banjo which I could visualise him strumming exuberantly. The easel was often set up in some part of the flat with a painting in the course of execution. The toilet was cluttered with badminton and tennis rackets and brochures about skiing resorts.

I longed for somewhere like the dingy waiting room of Dr Weissmann.

I thrust all this out of my mind and concentrated on how I would explain to Luc why I distrusted him.

He came for me wearing a hairy brown jacket with widely-spaced vertical and horizontal stripes of different colours.

'Why are you wearing that horrible jacket?' I jeered as we sat down.

'I think you've already seen it,' he answered mildly.

'Oh no, not that one. I wouldn't have forgotten it,' I said with as much nastiness as I could muster. 'And these shoes make you look like a pimp,' I added for good measure. They were brown brogues with patches of beige canvas.

We sat without saying anything for a while.

Finally he broke the silence. 'What are you thinking about?'

'There's something I've been thinking about a lot, something that really bothers me. It's that I don't trust you, professionally I mean. I just don't have any confidence in you but I keep on coming because I'm tied to you emotionally. It's not doing me any good though. Quite the contrary.'

'But this is projection, this feeling of distrust you have. You don't trust yourself, you don't think you're capable of anything and you have a very low opinion of yourself so you project all these things onto me and end up thinking that you can't have any confidence in me.'

'I don't agree with you. First of all, you can't say that it's projection if I have valid grounds for saying that I don't trust you. And I do have grounds. I don't trust you because you often contradict yourself. You say black one day and white the next. Often the things you say don't stand up to any logical scrutiny and sometimes, when I point it out to you, you agree with me, so you can't deny it now. Sometimes, even, you come out with things which seem to me to be just pure rubbish.

'And another thing. You trot out this thing about projection as if you think that every time I make a negative comment about you I'm attributing to you a characteristic of myself – in other words, criticising you for a fault which is really mine and not yours. If you believe this then it's tantamount to saying that every opinion that anyone expresses about anyone else applies in reality to the person who's expressing the opinion and not to the person he's talking about. This is clearly nonsense. I'm sure that in some circumstances this phenomenon of projection does occur but you have to eliminate all the other possibilities first – such as, is it true? is the person just trying to be nasty? is there some kind of ulterior motive? and so on – before finally deciding that what's being said is, in fact, projection.'

'But you do trust me. If you didn't trust me your reason wouldn't allow you to be so entrenched in this state of emotional dependence on me.'

'No, I don't think you're right. First of all, the state of emotional dependence has nothing to do with reason. It's just a function of my emotional needs and disposition. Anyway, what about the expression *"Le coeur a ses raisons que la raison ne connaît pas,"* * which you're always quoting to me? In any case, you keep on telling me that the feelings I have aren't really about you, they're about some other person from my past that you represent. Whether or not I trust you, Luc Landau, as a therapist, doesn't make any difference to the feelings I have about this other person who's temporarily incorporated into your persona.'

'But you're so caught up in this emotional state that your reason is suspended at the moment.'

'You've just contradicted yourself again. You said two minutes ago that I did trust you because if I didn't my reason wouldn't allow me to be so bogged down with you emotionally. Now you're saying that my reasoning powers have been deactivated. If this statement is true then it invalidates what you said previously.'

The conversation bumbled on along similar lines. I got more and more frustrated. No matter what I said to prove the illogicality of what he was saying, he came up with an even more illogical defence. As so often before when talking with Luc, I had the impression that our conversations only complicated matters. Even the simplest things took on a complexity which was impossible to unravel.

---

* The heart has its reasons that reason knows nothing of.

After I left that day I decided that I wouldn't go back again. I didn't know how I was going to manage not to, I just knew I had to try. The intellectual inconsistencies were driving me crazy, as was the fact that my intellectual position was at total variance with my emotional state.

A couple of days later I made an appointment with Dr Grosjean. If I was going to leave Luc I needed back-up support from someone else. What I wanted, ideally, was to go through the whole relationship with Luc with someone else, from beginning to end, so that I could get it into some kind of proper perspective and convince myself fully of the futility and irrationality of it all.

Later that afternoon, around the time for my usual appointment with Luc, I began to feel sick, weak and dizzy. I went to bed and was afraid to get out of it again. It was as if I was an embryo. I had been aborted and the bed was my incubator. Although I had decided to leave him, I picked up the phone and called Luc. Lying in my bed I talked to him. I told him about not wanting to see him any more and I also told him about being an aborted embryo, confined to an incubator. I continued, 'But no matter how I feel, there's just no point in carrying on. It doesn't make any sense. What's the purpose of it all? And what's your role in it? What's the point of all these years of study you've done when you don't actually do anything? You're totally inert. What's the point of it?'

'To allow you to use me as an object for your fantasies.'

'But that's the problem. My whole waking life is crowded out with these fantasies. There's no room for anything else.'

'That's what we have to analyse.'

'But it's just not working. Nothing is any clearer. Things are only getting worse. I want to stop.'

'You're not ready to stop yet. If you stop now you'll only have more problems to cope with.'

I was unconvinced. His last remark was emotional blackmail, but I knew that, in spite of myself, I was very susceptible to it.

'You still have an appointment the day after tomorrow,' he said. 'I'll be waiting for you. Come if you want to.'

The following day I went to see Dr Grosjean. I told him about recent events and explained what I wanted from him. It was clear from the beginning that he was not in the same receptive mood as on the previous occasion. Perhaps he was in a bad temper or, more likely, it may have been due to the fact that analysts generally don't like being asked to repair the damage done by others.

'I've been trying to think myself into a state of mind which leaves me no choice, at the rational level, but to reject him,' I said. 'For example, I'm very critical of him. I examine everything he says with a view to finding fault, and each fault I find is stored away in my memory and used to build a case for the prosecution, as it were.'

'Don't you find you do this with everyone?' he asked with a faintly jubilant look, as if he'd just identified a major defect in the structure of my psyche.

I considered this. 'No, I don't think so, and in any case I'm not just critical of him. I'm critical of my own behaviour in the situation and also of the theoretical grounds on which the therapy's based.'

I told him about the feeling of being aborted and my bed becoming an incubator.

'You're attracted by this sort of situation. This is the kind of thing you've been seeking with the therapist – an enclosed, non-verbal world where you can be protected. You stop seeing the man, so you try to get the same effect by taking refuge in your bed, shutting out the real world.'

He launched into a monologue in which he expanded at length on this theme and then, without stopping to sum up or ask for my reaction to all this, branched off to talk about the difficulties of doing a therapy in a foreign language, implying that I could hardly expect the whole business to be anything other than a disaster given that I wasn't doing it in my mother tongue. His discourse became increasingly rambling. He gesticulated wildly. I was finding it difficult to follow the train of his thought.

He stopped abruptly. 'That's about all I've got to say.' I paid him. 'I don't think I need show you to the door,' he said. 'You know the way.' He hadn't suggested making another appointment. Clearly he didn't want to take things any further.

As this emergency exit had been slammed in my face I felt I had no alternative but to return to Luc after all. Before going to my next appointment I drank half a bottle of wine, partly because going back again made me feel such a failure and partly because seeing him was so stressful.

I told him about my fruitless visit to Dr Grosjean and was strangely comforted to see that he was clearly indignant when I mentioned that Dr Grosjean had not accompanied me to the door when I left. I took this reaction to what he regarded as an insult as a sign that he cared about me.

We talked again about my feeling of being aborted.

'Were you born prematurely?'

'No, and I was never in an incubator. I was born at home, quite normally.'

'Well, in that case it doesn't make sense for you to say that when you're lying in bed you feel you're in an incubator. You can't know because you've never experienced it. It's not something you can be reliving because it never happened to you in the first place.'

'But that is how I feel. Or at least that's what I imagine being in an incubator is like. That's all I can say. It just happens to be the simile which comes to mind. And I'm supposed to say everything that comes into my mind, am I not? I thought that was the whole idea of analysis.

I can't help it if it doesn't make sense. Anyway, I thought that was your job – to make sense of it.'

As so often we seemed to be communicating in riddles and talking at cross-purposes.

I BEGAN TO feel that things were getting out of control again, that I was back to the point which I was at just before I went to see the woman at the Institute of Psychoanalysis, and that the reason for this was the failure of my attempt to leave Luc. I was spending a great deal of time in bed – the only place in which I felt safe; or at least relatively so, because even there I felt threatened. In fact these last months had been like a period of invalidity on account of the amount of time I'd spent in bed, either because I'd slept so little during the night, or because I'd taken so many sleeping pills to try to get to sleep, or because I had a hangover.

It looked as if I'd exhausted the various possibilities which I'd thought might help me out of the emotional trap I was in. There was a pressure building up in me, as if my mind, and my body too, were going to explode; there was a bomb which was going to go off inside me. I was constantly assaulted by waves of fear which left me feeling dizzy. I had a trembling feeling in my head, as if ripples were traversing my brain. And I had another strange feeling, the impression that my emotional reality was distorted so that it bore the same kind of relationship to what it normally was as a Picasso painting does to the scenes supposedly depicted. I tried to describe this to Luc but the words obviously meant nothing to him. This problem of communication was an added difficulty. As my psychological states were not, as far as I knew, part of a common pool of experience, or at least not one which is discussed, there were no words or expressions which I could use to make them recognisable. I therefore had to fall back on images or analogies which seemed either to perplex the people I was talking to, or be misconstrued by them.

I had a brain-storming session with myself to see if I could find some other way of escaping from Luc. I remembered Marion telling me that the person who had recommended Dr Weissmann had spent some time in a clinic at the beginning of her therapy and I thought that this might be the solution for me. It could serve as a kind of prison which would physically prevent me from going to see Luc. I could perhaps have some very strong drug treatment which would turn me into a zombie to such an extent that I wouldn't care any more about him. And presumably there would be some kind of therapeutic set-up which would induce in me a more reasonable frame of mind.

I phoned Dr Paget to ask what he thought of this.

'Yes, that's a good idea. It's just what you need. I'll make the necessary arrangements.' He fixed an appointment for me to go and see him about it.

I was relieved to think that there was now some concrete action I could take, but profoundly depressed to think that I had got myself into such an emotional predicament that I was going to have to be stashed away in a clinic. I cried hysterically when I saw Luc.

'Two years ago, before I started seeing you, I didn't have any need to go into a clinic. It's because of you that I'm in this terrible mess.'

'That's not quite true. You had problems then which were difficult to live with, but it's only now that you're beginning to realise the extent of their emotional impact on you.'

'But I could live with them before. When I think about all the people I've known I realise that I'm probably no worse than average as regards being neurotic. The only thing a bit different about me is that I probably find it more difficult to hide my neurosis, or my oddness, whatever you want to call it. Often I get feedback from people indicating that they find me a bit bizarre or eccentric, but it's not always a disadvantage. Sometimes it's seen as something quite positive. Give me back these problems now and if that's all I've got wrong with me I'll go away quite happily. But I can't because I can't cope with the emotional turmoil that's been brought about by my relationship with you.'

I had recently read *Les Jardiniers de la Folie*, by Edouard Zarifian, a well-known French psychiatrist. In the book he expressed the opinion that psychoanalysis should only be undertaken by the psychologically fit.

'He says that for the neurotic it can lead to madness or suicide,' I told Luc. 'I don't know if that's true in general but it certainly corresponds to my own case.'

He disagreed. 'You're strong, much stronger than you think.'

He was wrong. He must have been misreading something. The situation I was in with him had completely broken my spirit. Until that point in my life I'd always felt that, if nothing else, I was a survivor. I wasn't surviving any more.

'He also says that it can't be regarded as a therapy, but only as an existential experience. That's pretty much what I think. It doesn't actually bring about any changes. It's just something you experience, like a dream.'

'I don't think I agree with that. I think we can work towards change. And I think you should stop trying to invalidate our relationship by this process of critical reasoning that you constantly apply and try instead to understand what it is that binds you to me emotionally. You can let me help you understand this, and if you do this you'll find that you're setting yourself free from it.'

'No, you can't help me because you're not capable of it. All you do is harm me. And I can't set aside my reason because, in order to do that and to hand myself over in a state of complete vulnerability, I'd already have had to have used my reason to establish that the person was someone I could trust and not just any old idiot. That's what I can't do with you.'

Harsh and disagreeable words. But at another, more emotional, level I was reacting quite differently. His suggestion that he should help me work towards separation from him made me feel like a child being told by his parent that the best thing he could do for him was to find a nice orphanage to put him in.

For some time now my manner when talking with Luc had become increasingly childish, as if I was growing younger over the weeks. A strange feeling came over me as I was about to leave that day, making me feel as if I had been transported back in time to a very young age. I spoke to him in a whining voice, in English, tears running down my cheeks, 'I'm not well'.

'You're not well? You mean physically?'

'I'm going to be sick.' I felt as if I was going to vomit all over his desk.

'You're like a little child who's not well, who's been separated from its mother, perhaps.'

I was abruptly transported back to the real world. I no longer felt sick or as if I had the mind of a toddler. 'Stop talking crap,' I shouted angrily.

I lay awake most of the night, despite sleeping pills, in a state of inexpressible, ineffable pain. Going into a clinic now seemed the only solution left to me and if it didn't work I would have to kill myself. It didn't even seem like a decision I would make; it would simply be the inevitable result of what was happening, an inescapable destiny. In fact, I wouldn't even be killing myself because I was already dead – a zombie, a *mort-vivant*. This feeling of being propelled towards death was similar to the feeling I had had when I was compelled to phone Luc on those occasions when I had tried to stop seeing him. It was as if some outside force took over and made me do it.

Another thing that pushed me towards dying was that I so strongly needed to give expression to the feelings that had been elicited, or brought into being, by my relationship with Luc and the only act which I felt could correspond with their intensity was to die. I would quite literally die for him, or at least for what I felt about him.

At the same time, details of the real world would pop into my mind, drawing me back from the brink. I remembered reading that for Schopenhauer, the funniest thing he could think of was a tangent to a circle. He had said that he could think of nothing more exquisitely amusing than the idea of a line approaching a circle only to recede from it again. Although I myself didn't think the tangent to a circle in the least bit funny, I found Schopenhauer's view of it so perfectly enchanting that I didn't want to withdraw from a world where such notions could exist. And I suddenly became very attached to certain possessions. Comical pictures which till then I had barely noticed because I was so used to them struck me once again with their endearing absurdity. Items from countries I had visited reactivated my interest in these places. To my surprise I found that I was still able to feel delight when a new series of *I'm Sorry I Haven't a Clue* started on Radio Four. But this was all in the realm of ideas. There was nothing in my emotional life which had a similar effect on me.

I tried to think of other reasons why I shouldn't die, and how absurd it was for me to feel so bad when there were so many outrageous, frightful problems in the world. It didn't make any difference because I didn't believe I was in that world any longer. I was in another universe, and I didn't see how I could get back into the real one.

I spoke to Luc again about these things. I was vituperative and malevolent.

'There are two possibilities left for me now: going into a clinic or killing myself. I think it's fifty-fifty. And I want you to know that if I kill myself, each time that you fuck with that woman my dead body will slip in between you. And if you have a child it'll be conceived across my dead body. And I'm going to come and see that woman again and repeat to her what I've just said.'

I thought he looked a bit appalled but he pulled himself together.

'You're talking like a small child who's angry with its parents.'

'No, I'm not. It's because I want to get my revenge on you, personally, for not providing me with what I should be able to expect from a therapist. What you've done is unforgivable. You manoeuvred me into a situation in which I'm totally dependent on you and then you deprived me of the possibility of carrying it through to its conclusion. I'm stuck, like an astronaut in a spaceship that's gone out of control and gone hurtling off into outer space till eventually he just dies of inanition.'

When I went to see Dr Paget the clinic idea had to be abandoned as it turned out that the only facilities provided were those of a kind of rest home, with drugs and an occasional brief chat with a doctor.

As usual I had the impression that Dr Paget was uncomfortable about my problem – probably because he felt impotent in the face of it – but I wanted to force him into doing something about it, or at least telling me what he really thought. After all, he was a psychiatrist, not just a drug-dispensing machine.

'The way I feel, total dependence on a therapist, it's a well-known syndrome. How is it that therapists can encourage this state of affairs to come about without having any means of clearing up the mess when things go wrong for whatever reason, as they have done in my case? Why isn't there even any advice that can be given to the patient in these circumstances?'

'But there is – stop the therapy.'

'No, this sort of answer won't do. What about the situation when you just can't stop because you know that you'll die if you do? And if I died you couldn't even say that it was suicide as such. If I stopped seeing Dr Landau I would just stop living. Whether it was because of some action I took myself or whether I simply stopped breathing, it's all the same. The fact is that I'm unable to live without him. This is the literal truth. It's not a manner of speaking. He's destroyed something in me. It's as if the springs of my mind had been broken.'

'I think you should still carry on looking for another psychotherapist,' he said rather weakly.

I mentioned having thought of the possibility of doing some kind of group therapy as it would provide me with a situation in which I could express myself without the danger of becoming dependent. He picked up the phone, rang someone and tried to arrange to have me taken on in some group. I didn't know what or where or with whom, but it turned out that there was no vacancy. I felt that he was clutching at straws. As that had failed, he said that he would speak about me to a colleague at a psychiatric hospital and told me to make an appointment to see this person.

'What for?' I asked.

'To get an opinion, an orientation,' he said vaguely.

It seemed like a buck-passing exercise. But what else could he do, given that nothing could be done with the buck? It was more like a game of pass-the-parcel.

I felt increasingly desperate. I didn't know what to do or where to turn. Each day I managed to get through without killing myself seemed like the achievement of a miracle. The most frustrating thing was that I didn't understand anything about what was going on. Perhaps I had been transported back to some infantile or embryonic stage of development, but thinking about this didn't help in any way as it was pure hypothesis. I had no idea if it was true. And if it was true, then it was as if I had travelled backwards in a time machine and been left stranded there. There was no return journey. I felt very insecure with all these psychotherapists. They didn't seem to have much idea of what they were doing. I had the impression that in the 'psy' domain, knowledge was about as far advanced as medicine at the time of Hippocrates: a minimum of facts, a number of wild theories, and great deal of groping around in the dark, doing far more harm than good.

More out of curiosity than anything else, I made an appointment with Dr Paget's colleague. I saw him at the hospital, in what seemed like an unnecessarily medical environment. He was a shapeless man with porcine features and a boorish manner.

'What brings you?' he grunted.

'Dr Paget suggested that I should see you. He said he would talk to you about it. Have you spoken to him?'

'No.' He shrugged unenthusiastically. 'Tell me what the problem is.'

I told him the story briefly. He screwed up his face and strained forward as if he had difficulty understanding. I began to feel embarrassed about my foreign accent. Perhaps he had no idea what I was saying. But I didn't generally have this problem. Perhaps he was deaf.

'And why do you want to see me about this?' he asked with ill-humoured perplexity.

'Well, that's what I wondered myself when Dr Paget suggested it, but he thought that it would be useful to get another opinion.'

'What do you expect me to say? You just have to sort out the problem with the therapist that you're already with.'

'But I can't, that's the problem. It's obviously getting nowhere, and for months now it's been wrecking my life. I'm drugged to the eyeballs, most of the time pissed out of my mind, incapable of leading any kind of social life, barely able to work, and feel that I've gone totally crazy. This can't be a good thing.'

'Go to someone else then. That's the obvious thing to do. People are changing therapists every day. That's all I can say. What do you expect me to do?'

He let me go after barely twenty minutes and I rushed out into the street, relieved to have escaped so quickly from this disagreeably saturnine character.

SINCE MY FIRST visit to Dr Grosjean I had again been caught up frequently in sexual fantasies about Luc, but now their character had changed significantly compared with those I had had previously. Although sexually aroused I no longer felt like a woman; instead I was a child, perhaps a baby even. Luc was still the object of my desire but very often there was no genital activity taking place between us. I just longed for him intensely and felt wildly stimulated by this state of longing. On one occasion I spent a day in bed constantly moving in and out of quasi-hallucinatory states in which I was an infant in an adult's arms, powerfully excited sexually and continually on the brink of orgasm.

I wanted to talk to Luc about all this but my lack of confidence in him prevented me doing so. Even more than talking about it objectively, I wanted somehow to transpose these fantasies of infantile sexuality into scenes which I could act out with him in the way I acted out my aggression, but something inhibited me. In any case part of me dismissed it all as something not to be taken seriously. I told myself that these fantasies had simply arisen out of notions which had been put into my head by everything that I'd been reading about psychoanalysis and theories of infantile sexuality, and that none of it had anything to do with my emotional reality or childhood experience.

The shift towards this infantile desire made no difference to the jealousy I felt about Luc's woman. As far as this was concerned, my mind was as sensitive as a body with third-degree burns. I recoiled from anything relating to sex or women's bodies. I turned my head away if I found myself walking past displays of underwear in shops as it made me think of her undressing in front of him. Newspaper kiosks constituted a similar danger as there were so many magazine covers showing half-naked women or referring to articles about sex to be found inside. Television advertising was a minefield as there were so many scenes involving young couples, sex and romance. The sight of my own body was intolerable as it made me think of hers and what he did with it; I had to avert my eyes when undressing or having a shower. None of the things Luc and the woman did together could bear contemplation.

One morning I woke up feeling simply awful physically. There was no obvious reason for it, and it wasn't a hangover as I hadn't had a drink the previous day. For a couple of hours I couldn't even open my eyes as it caused such acute, dazzling discomfort. Eventually I had to get up to go to the toilet. My limbs were almost unmanageable, like cotton wool. My head was swimming. Afterwards, when I was lying down again, the dizziness continued. The sensations were exactly the same as those I remembered experiencing when I was being injected with an anaesthetic, just before losing consciousness.

By midday the feelings had abated sufficiently for me to find the energy to try and work out what it was all about. It was so weird that I thought that it must have some connection with my psychological state. For some reason I thought of a short story by Oscar Wilde which I had once read. It was about a person who came into existence, not as a baby, but as an old man. The story described the events of his life which, of course, were in the reverse order of a normal life. It finished by him being born, going back into the womb and then, at the end, disappearing into a void, which was the period preceding conception. I had the rather fanciful notion that it was a similar situation to the one I was in. I was travelling back in time. I was perhaps in the process of being sucked back into the womb. Then I decided that this was more nonsense due to reading too many books about psychoanalysis. I was like a child who terrorises itself by reading ghost stories and then can't sleep at night because of the images conjured up.

Nevertheless I felt frighteningly bizarre. I needed to talk about it. I decided to phone Luc. It was a Wednesday, the day on which he would normally be at the hospital. I called his flat first to check with the answering machine which always gave details of where he could be contacted. The phone rang a few times. Then it was picked up.

'Hallo.' The voice sprang out of the receiver; sharp, clear – and female. The voice of the woman who shared Luc's bed. It affected something in my mind in the way a singer, hitting a certain note, can shatter a glass chandelier. I hung up and cowered deeper into the bed.

By the next day I had recovered physically but was, if anything, even more profoundly depressed. I was demented with grief. It was terrifying. Nothing touched me, nothing was of any concern to me. It was as if my mind had been changed by a drug, but it was worse than that because the effects of drugs wear off. I felt dazed and stunned with pain and I didn't know why. If I had known why, I would at least have known how to start doing something about it, but how could I find a solution when I didn't even know the nature of the problem?

I communicated some of this morbid feeling to Luc in the childish manner that I now consistently adopted with him. 'I'm going to tell you what I'm going to do with you. Do you want to know? Do you want me to tell you what I'm going to do?' I felt about three years old.

He said nothing but gave me an encouraging look. I moved on to his knee, put my arms round him and, with my face against his, I whispered, *'Je vais faire la mort avec vous.'* There was something very satisfying about being able to say this to him. It was both seductive, because of the word play *'faire la mort/faire l'amour'*, and menacing.

'What do you mean?'

'I mean I'm going to kill myself because of you, and I'm going to kill myself here in your flat – and it's all your fault,' I shouted spitefully.

Nothing was said for a few moments and then, 'Do you know the expression *"la petite mort"*?' he asked.

'No.'

'It's sometimes used when referring to orgasm. Perhaps that's what you mean when you say that's what you want to do with me.'

I didn't say anything but I felt rather put out. It was as if he'd taken the edge off my viciousness by interpreting what I'd said in this way, though in fact he was wrong. Such a thought hadn't crossed my mind. We sat in silence for a while.

A saxophonist was playing at the other side of the street. The strains of 'Yesterday' came floating in through the open window. The words ran through my head, but for me, yesterday, when troubles seemed, relatively speaking, so far away, was all the days before the day I stumbled into the hornet's nest of my relationship with Luc.

'You've never identified what I represent for you – mother, father, lover, or what?' he asked, disturbing my thoughts.

I considered the question, switching back into adult mode to reply.

'It needn't necessarily be just one thing. A therapist can represent different things at different times. But to do so, he has to be able to present himself as a kind of blank screeen to the patient and this is what you can't do because your professional environment is invaded by your private life. Often I just begin to react to you in certain ways and then I can't because our relationship is entirely swamped by your identity as the lover of that woman. That's what you represent for me and nothing else. Your reality is too present.'

'Resistance!' The word was shouted out triumphantly, the battle cry of the therapist. 'This is because you're afraid of what I could represent for you.'

'Bullshit!'

Then I allowed myself to examine the question more closely. In a way he was a bit like a kaleidoscope for me as my perceptions of him could vary so much and so rapidly. Just at that moment it occurred to me that he was like a teddy bear – something which I could cuddle and hug but from which I didn't expect any communication at a thinking level. I looked at him closely and decided that he was more like a golliwog than a teddy bear, with his swarthy appearance and the mass of black springy curls. He reminded me of the golliwog that I had had as a child, and just at that instant the love that I had felt for that golliwog was reactivated and I experienced it with all the force and intensity which I had felt for it so many years before. It just about broke my heart to think that the doll, lost some time in the distant past, was gone for ever. I felt that I loved it desperately.

'For me you're a golliwog,' I told him, 'because of your hair, and because you're something I can play with but which doesn't have a brain.' I kept the other feelings to myself. It would have embarrassed me to express them as they seemed so mawkish.

That night I dreamt about my brother Jack – four years older than me and my only sibling. The events of the dream were of no particular interest, but the next morning I remembered something I hadn't thought of for years, probably not at all since the time of its occurrence. Jack used to use my golliwog as a hostage when I was being tiresome. He would threaten to hit it unless I behaved in the way he wanted. I again felt the intense love for the golliwog and relived the total powerlessness I used to feel when he said he was going to hurt it.

Luc

MY JEALOUSY AT this time was very strongly channelled into anger. I had fantasies about wrecking the flat, smashing things, breaking the windows, going into the bedroom and destroying things belonging to the woman. I also toyed obsessively with the idea of hiding myself in the bedroom, perhaps in a cupboard or under the bed, and witnessing his sexual relationship with the woman. I had the notion that, as the sexual act seems so absurd if you think about it dispassionately, it would reduce everything to ordinary proportions if I could actually see it. I would spring out of my hiding place while they were frenetically engaged in their sexual activity, laugh, and then walk away, cured. The spell would be broken.

But most of all I wanted to go into that bedroom, lie on the bed and act as if I belonged there. I always hated walking the last bit of the street just before I entered his building because in doing so I had to walk under the bedroom window on the first floor above. Its shutters were always closed, no matter what the time of day or the season. This irritated me as I saw it as a sign of paranoia on Luc's part, as if he imagined that his patients were going to congregate down on the pavement, spying into the room with the aid of giant periscopes in an effort to find out what was going on inside. But the truth was that I desperately wanted to know what went on inside, and the shuttered windows only served to heighten the mystery and my feeling of exclusion.

One day when I arrived he was in the bedroom. I heard voices. It sounded like the radio but I told myself that it was the woman. I refused to speak to him when we went into the office. I was now convinced that the woman was in the bedroom. In order to check this out, I left the office to go to the toilet, my ear cocked towards the bedroom in order to detect the slightest sound. There was none, but this did not diminish my obsessive suspicions.

'That woman's in the bedroom,' I snarled when I went back.

'No, there's nobody.'

'Yes, there is. I'm going to see.' I ran out of the office. He came after me and grabbed me just as I reached the bedroom door. I cowered petulantly in the corner, pulling away from him, but not too hard. I knew that if I really wanted to I could break free and go bursting into the room but I was afraid to; afraid that she might be there, in which case I wouldn't know what to do, and afraid that Luc might throw me out altogether.

I allowed myself to be dragged back into the office.

'I want to see if that woman's there.'

'No, you want to see my bed, that's what you want.'

I pouted sullenly, but he was right. I did feel drawn, like a magnet, to the bed at the other side of the closed door. I flounced around in childish ill-temper on the couch, punching the cushions and turning my back on him.

'What a shabby old pair of trousers you're wearing,' I snapped, desperate to find some means of offending him.

'Yes, they are rather creased,' he agreed.

Then I started to howl with indignation, accusing him of having let me find out things which it was intolerable for me to be witness to.

'It's true that you're suffering in your relationship with me, but you've always suffered. This relationship can help you to stop suffering. And now that you know that there's a woman in my life it can allow you to communicate with me intimately without being afraid that I'm going to penetrate you with my penis.'

'I don't believe it! I just don't believe that you can say such a thing! I've never heard such fucking crap! In the first place it would never, ever, enter my head that you could possibly even consider wanting to penetrate me with your fucking little cock, and even if it did, I wouldn't be afraid of it. It's the one thing I want more than anything else in the world. What the hell are you talking about, for Christ's sake? And even if I was afraid of this in some strange fantasy part of my subconscious that I'm not yet aware of, it's not the presence of a real woman in the real world that would make any difference.'

It infuriated me because it showed such a lack of understanding. If he really thought that I was afraid of sex with him, or with any other man for that matter, he was barking completely up the wrong tree. It was maddening to hear such bullshit, to be unable to convince him of its wrongness and to know that I was in such a state of emotional slavery to someone whose mind was working along such erroneous lines. Worst of all, I began to fear that I might even end up one day being brought round to his point of view. I was beginning to feel like a political prisoner locked away in a psychiatric hospital: impotent, completely at my captor's mercy, and in danger of being browbeaten into believing anything he wanted to say, no matter how absurd.

As a last resort I decided to have one more go with drugs. I still had my last prescription from Dr Paget which I had been too discouraged to try at the time. Nothing else he'd given me had worked, so I didn't see why these should. Nevertheless I started taking them. On the third day I realised the minute I woke up that something was different. I felt quite stimulated and had an energy that I hadn't felt in myself for months. The feeling stayed with me. Over the next few days I found myself again able to do mundane things like shopping and cleaning the flat which, till then, had been like insurmountable obstacles. I could also read, watch television and listen to the radio, giving these things most of my attention instead of the cursory glance and half an ear that I'd got used to. Communicating with other people was less of a problem.

The drug was affecting me quite strongly. It was like taking a combination of amphetamines and cannabis; I was slightly hyper-excited and spaced out. But, after all these months of what had seemed like a bad LSD trip, I wasn't complaining. Nevertheless I felt insecure. I knew I was being buoyed up by the drug but I didn't know how long it was going to work or when I would be cast back down into my previous state. It was as if I was being swept across mountainous chasms in an unreliable old cable car. Not only might it collapse and go tumbling down at any moment, it was also a shaky ride, with lurches, stops and starts, and vertigo. At the same time there was something intoxicating about the height and the speed, or in other words, about the distance which had been put between me and my emotional problems and my new-found ability to cope with things again.

But there was one thing I still couldn't cope with, and that was the idea of leaving Luc. I tried out the idea, thinking that in my new state of mind I might feel differently about it. My mind veered away from it with the kind of nauseous lurching of the consciousness which precedes a faint. It was as impossible as a paraplegic moving without a wheelchair.

Not only could I not leave him, I was still as sensitive as ever to everything that happened within our relationship.

Shortly after I had started to feel better he happened to mention that he was Jewish. We spoke about this for a bit. I was violently anti-Zionist and wanted to be sure that he did not support the status quo in Israel. The question had barely been broached when I suddenly remembered hearing once that Jews were reputed to have particularly satisfying and uninhibited sex lives. My rage and jealousy about the woman were renewed. It wasn't just an ordinary, average sexual relationship that I had to be jealous of now. I wondered furiously what he actually did with her. Even things that some people considered way-out, like oral sex and various acrobatic positions, were really just standard practice, so what did Jews do that made it so much better? Whatever it was, he did it with her, and my fury knew no bounds. I hurled myself flat on the couch and screamed and punched the cushions. I didn't tell him what it was all about. Saying it would have made it more real. As long as I didn't verbalise it I could keep the idea at bay.

When I'd exhausted my rage I turned round, lying on my back. I stretched out my legs and placed them across his knees. I shifted around, fidgeting with my legs, moving them about till finally my right foot was placed on his genitals. We were talking again about the state of Israel; he didn't change the subject. I moved my foot rhythmically. It quickly produced an erection. He stared at me impassively.

'You told me that you didn't get an erection with your patients,' I said accusingly.

'No, I didn't. I said that we're not here for that purpose. We're here for one thing only, to deal with your problems, and any reactions or desires that I might have inadvertently are of no relevance.'

The hard penis under my foot was bigger than I had expected. I flung myself back onto the couch, again beside myself with rage. For the second time that day I was confronted with something I didn't want to know. Irrationally I felt that this big penis made him an even better lover, enabling him to give more pleasure to the woman in his bed.

I turned my head to look round at him. He was sucking the end of a pen.

'Why are you sucking that? It's because you're not smoking at the moment. You can't bear to be deprived of your oral satisfaction.'

'You say that because you want to suck my cock but you don't dare admit it.'

'Rubbish. Of course I dare. I don't need to talk about pens if I want you to know that I want to suck your cock. I've never made any secret about the things I want to do with you.'

'I think you feel uncomfortable about the fact that I let you say and do all these things to me without imposing any restraints.'

I didn't say anything because it was a question that had occurred to me and I didn't know the answer to it yet. Most of all, I wondered why he seemed to be offering himself to me as something resembling a cross between a punchbag and a passive gigolo. But I didn't want the answer from him. I wanted to work it out for myself.

He carried on without being asked. 'If I let you act out a lot of your feelings it's because you have such difficulty in verbalising them. By expressing them physically you can let them come to the surface and then you can recognise their existence.'

Was this the answer I would have worked out for myself? Probably not.

I returned to the question of Zionism the next time I saw him.

'What really bothers me is that I can't believe that there exists a Jew who isn't, no matter how deep down, to some extent a supporter of Israel.'

'Oh, I don't think you're quite right there. But in any case, when it came into being in 1948 all the countries were in favour of it, including Britain.'

'There you are, a perfect example of the sloppiness of your thinking.' I pounced on him. 'What do you mean by "all the countries"? For a start, only the member countries of the United Nations were involved and a number of them either voted against or abstained. In any case, even if all the countries in the world had voted for it, that wouldn't necesssarily have made it right. There could be any number of reasons for doing so – self-interest, emotional blackmail, lots of things which don't stand up to scrutiny if you think about it from the standpoint of what's morally right or wrong. And the fact that the British were in favour is totally irrelevant to this discussion. Your only reason for mentioning them must be that because I'm British you think that I'm in some way an accomplice to what happened. Or perhaps you think it's disloyal of me to criticise something which was agreed to by my country? Whatever the reason, the remark is nonsensical. You probably think I'm splitting hairs, but this is typical of your way of talking and the thing is that everything said in therapy is supercharged with meaning, every word is important, so you can't just talk through a hole in your head and hope that no one will notice.'

He agreed that the remark was ill-advised.

I had him at a disadvantage and I pressed home. 'What puzzles me is that to look at, you seem quite an intelligent person. You don't have the vacant look that stupid people normally have, but you are stupid. Are you angry with me for saying that?'

'No, why should I be angry?'

'I'd be angry if somebody said things like that to me, but if you're not, that's fine. Another thing, I've often been struck by the stupidity of things you say but I've never been struck by anything that seemed to be intelligent or perceptive.'

I'd been talking in a vicious, spiteful tone, like a child out for revenge. Then I realised that I fully believed what I was saying. I felt nervous and was afraid of alienating him but I had to go on.

'I'm supposed to say everything that comes into my mind, am I not?'

'Yes.'

'But I'm afraid of offending you.'

'You can say anything. I'm not here to be offended.'

'Rubbish! That neutrality that therapists talk about is just a myth.'

'I'm listening.'

'It's true that I think you're not particularly intelligent. Something that bothers me a lot and that really impedes communication is that I think I'm more intelligent than you. I don't want a therapist who's less intelligent than me. It should be the other way round. You often say that we should be analysing my feelings, but how? You don't have an analytical type of mind.'

I told him how I felt when I saw the chess set in the sitting room. 'I just can't imagine you playing chess. If you played with me I'd make mincemeat of you.'

He listened in silence. 'You must always say what you think,' he said when I had finished. 'Don't worry about the effect it might have on me.' He patted my knee as he said this, as if reassuring a child. I felt affronted because, for once, I'd been talking to him in a wholly adult capacity.

MY FANTASY relationship with Luc was increasingly an infantile one. I had fantasies of being like a baby, carried under his arm, kicking, struggling and screaming hysterically in a paroxysm of anger. It was a fantasy that I got pleasure out of, like a sexual one, but it didn't diminish the rage and jealousy I felt about the woman. Occasionally I had the fleeting feeling that 'sex is just for big people', an activity that I was unjustly excluded from, and I would almost burst with fury. These regression experiences were very similar in nature to things which had happened to me under the influence of LSD, when I felt I had been transported back in time to the age of about three.

This situation wasn't purely restricted to fantasy. My behaviour when I was with him was also extremely infantile. I was like a child reacting with an adult: being difficult, sulking, having tantrums, shrieking and thumping with rage, writhing around all over him in a demonstration of affection, wriggling down into the refuge of his arms. When I spoke to him it was as a kind of child-adult half-cast, and often what was said didn't seem to make much sense.

On this occasion I sulked for a while when I arrived, following a pattern which was becoming quite usual. I sat on the couch with my back to him, my arms round the cushions, turning to look at him every now and again, alternately reproachful, accusing, resentfully pouting, or with an expression of injured innocence like a three-year-old. I could sense him straining the muscles of his face in an effort not to laugh. I suppose there was something very comical in watching a grown woman acting like a toddler.

I noticed he was wearing a black linen jacket and a florid shirt.

'New clothes again,' I said nastily. 'You don't stint yourself.'

'Neither do you,' he replied, eyeing my trousers meaningfully. He obviously thought they were rather chic. They were from Marks and Spencer's children's department.

'Misinterpretation!' I snarled. 'I see you've had your hair cut,' I carried on. 'Trying to make yourself a pretty little boy. Well, let me tell that you're uglier than ever when your hair's short.'

Now that some of my bile had been spent in this manner I leaned over and settled myself on top of him with my head on his chest. As I did so my eyes fell on a letter which was lying on his desk. I saw just a few words, but it was enough to let me know that it was from a patient. I leapt back as if scalded. 'That's a letter from a patient. Take it away. I don't want to see it,' I yelped.

'Ah yes, you're quite right.' He moved it out of sight.

I was swept up in paroxysm of wrath at the thought of another patient writing to him. I wanted to be the only person who wrote to him. In fact, I wanted to be the only person he ever saw. I started to scream and howl, shrieks alternating with incoherent sentences, my arms tightly round his neck. 'Nobody else can write to you – I want to be the only person – tell them they can't send you letters.' I screamed again. I bit his ear.

When the worst of the storm was over he questioned me about it.

'Do you love me?'

'No.'

'Do you hate me?'

'No ... I want you to love me.' My voice was already hoarse and squeaky from the bruised vocal chords.

'You want me to love you more than the others?'

'No, not *more* than the others, *only* me. I want you to love *only* me.'

He looked as if he was starting to laugh at my childishness. 'It's not funny,' I roared. 'I can feel a wave of anger rising up again. I'm going to scream. And when I go home I'm going to have to drink all the time because that's what I do when I've got feelings of uncontrollable anger that I have to extinguish. Now I'm going to be angry all the time when I think about that letter.'

'No, you're not. You're angry now because when you're here you're a child, but when you go away you'll return to being an adult again and you won't be angry any more.'

It was true that my anger seemed to evaporate afterwards; either that, or it had gone into cold storage to be brought out again at some later date. I was exhausted when I got home and, although it was only early afternoon, I had to go to bed and stay there for the rest of the day. But the screaming had made me feel better and I wanted to do more of it. I felt that if I could just scream loud enough and long enough I might feel better altogether.

Odi et amo. Quare id faciam, fortasse requiris.
Nescio, sed fieri sentio et excrucior.*

I was so struck by this couplet when I studied it at school years ago, so seemingly rudimentary and yet so poetic, that I still knew it by heart. I felt I knew exactly what Catullus was expressing and identified with him totally. It applied now. Did that mean that I had lied to Luc when he interrogated me about love and hate? Not really, but if I just transformed the words slightly and substituted the notions of rage and desire for hate and love then the very essence of my relationship with him was distilled in those lines.

I felt ready for something momentous to happen after that last session with him. He could have plucked me like a ripe plum from a tree, but he didn't know how to. Or perhaps he didn't realise that now was the season.

It was noisy outside. I asked Luc to close the window. He said

---

*   I hate and I love. Perhaps you ask why I do so.
     I do not know, but I feel these things and am tortured.

that he preferred not to because of his cigarette smoke. The mention of cigarettes reminded me of a fragment of a dream I had once had. I described it. 'You put a cigarette in my mouth. That's all that happened in the dream, nothing else. But I know what you're going to say. Go on, say it. I can see it coming.'

He refused to be drawn into this.

'If you're so sure of my interpretation, tell me yourself.'

'You're going to say that it wasn't really a cigarette, that what it represented was your tiny little cock.'

'You're the one who's saying it.'

'Yes, but I'm saying it because I know that that's what you would say.'

'Not necessarily. Perhaps you dreamt that I put a cigarette in your mouth because you think that I encourage you to do things that are bad for you. You stopped smoking a long time ago and you don't want to start again.'

'Smart guy!'

I ground to a halt. Things weren't going as planned. I had expected to take up where I had left off the previous time, I wanted to get back into the full swing of my screaming, but the atmosphere was now quite different.

He changed the subject and started talking about my anger, very objectively as if it was something he was examining under a microscope. I didn't want to talk about my anger; I wanted to express it. The gist of what he was saying was that I got pleasure out of expressing anger with him.

'Well, yes, but only insofar as being relieved of something which creates stress is a pleasure. So it's a negative pleasure rather than a positive one. It's like needing to go to the toilet when your bladder's absolutely bursting and then when you can actually let go you do experience it as a kind of pleasure. That's what I feel like when I'm aggressive with you. I've had all this tension building up for ages and sometimes I let some of it out and it's good. What's wrong with that?'

'I'm not saying there's anything wrong with it. But you have to see that there's something pleasurable in it for you.'

'I do see it! I'm saying it's like having a pee when you're desperate.'

'You're here to analyse and understand things, not to live them.'

He was making me feel guilty. I began to feel embarrassed about all the screaming I'd done the previous time because I felt he was trying to tell me that it was all just an act which, perversely, I got some kind of kick out of. I was frustrated because he seemed to think that I expressed anger purely for reasons of hedonistic gratification rather than on account of some deeper need. I was confused and perplexed. His words and behaviour comprised so many inconsistencies that I didn't know where I was.

'So you don't like it when I shout?' I asked him.

'No, I don't,' he admitted.

This didn't tie in with what he'd said on previous occasions when he seemed to be actively encouraging me to express things in any way I wanted. Perhaps the neighbours had been complaining.

I was beginning to get very angry again but I had to express it differently now; less flamboyantly. So, feeling spiteful, I tore the cover of one of the books lying on his desk. This seemed to annoy him much more than screaming would have done. I switched back into adult mode and tried again to discuss my need to express anger and the way I felt when I did so but the lines of communication were down. I gave up.

'You're bored today,' I accused him.

'I'm not here to be bored. I'm here to work.'

'That's got nothing to do with it. Working's not necessarily got anything to do with not being bored, and it certainly doesn't preclude it. Don't try and tell me that during all the hours of the week that you work you're never at any time bored. You say that because you're such a goody-goody. You're trying to imply that you're so interested in your work and devoted to it that you can't be bored while you're doing it. Bullshit! Fucking hypocrite!'

Having got that off my chest I decided to make more of an effort to talk to him at a rational level. I started by telling him about my eating habits which had been getting increasingly bizarre. For some time I had been finding it difficult to eat most kinds of food, even though I often felt hungry. On the other hand I was compulsively stuffing myself with peanuts and apples, which were about the only thing I could swallow without wanting to vomit. The inside of my mouth was beginning to get raw and swollen from the salty nuts. He asked a few idle questions and then changed the subject abruptly to ask why I wore my mother's wedding ring. I replied briefly and returned to the peanuts. He persisted in his questioning about the wedding ring. As we were now talking about two entirely different things the conversation lost momentum and eventually petered out.

I felt let down. It was as if my attempt to behave like an adult and take the whole business seriously had been ignored. For want of anything better to say I started insulting him about his appearance.

'You look even skinnier than ever today. You must weigh less than me. Well, at least that way you don't crush women when you screw them. But no, that's not true, because you don't screw women at all. Do you know how I know that you don't screw? It's because your cock isn't long enough.' I had fully retreated to a position of petty, spiteful childishness.

'Aren't you expressing a frustration you feel about yourself when you say that?'

'What do you mean?'

'Well, don't little girls feel that their penis is too short, the little bit of clitoris that they have?'

'Crap, Freudian rubbish,' I shouted, though I didn't know why I felt compelled to react like this. I did, in fact, believe that there was a validity in these ideas. I had already told Luc about a vivid memory I had of experiencing penis envy myself. I was about three, in the toilet, and trying to urinate by standing in front of it like a boy instead of sitting down. I remember feeling convinced at that moment that 'it' would grow. It just had to grow. I didn't know when, but it would. Soon, I hoped. The idea that it might not was simply inconceivable.

'I wanted to talk about other things today,' I grumbled, 'but as usual you always bring the subject round to sex. You're never happy unless we're talking about your little cock. Perhaps you think that if you talk about it enough, then it'll grow.'

I had fallen right into the trap. This was further grist to the Freudian mill.

'Well, no. It's not little boys who want their penis to grow. It's little girls.'

I stared at him, dumbly indignant, at a loss to know what to say. While I sat saying nothing my eyes kept on being drawn towards his hair. I felt a compulsion to pull it. I finally did so, tugging and yanking and pulling his head towards me. I eventually tired of this.

'Why do you pull my hair when you really want to stroke it?' he asked.

'I don't!'

'Did you notice that when you were pulling my hair you were pulling me towards you in a particular way. It wasn't just aggression – you were pulling my head towards a particular part of your body as if you wanted a special kind of caress.' He had expressed himself very delicately. Just as he said this I realised that it was true and it embarrassed me. I was angry with him for saying it.

Suddenly my eye was caught by a schmaltzy china ornament on one of the shelves behind him, a couple of black kittens curled up mawkishly in a basket. 'Why on earth have you got these awful kittens?' I roared, delighted to have found something which I could get at him about. It was also an opportunity to change the subject. 'How can you put such a thing on your shelves? It's so kitsch.'

'Well yes, I'm inclined to agree ...' he started, looking amused.

'Why then ... ?'

'Oh, that would be breaching professional confidence,' he said, teasingly, and I realised that a patient had given it to him – a present. We fell about laughing. The thing was really terrible and looked completely out of place in the otherwise trendily intellectual decor.

'Can't you hide it and just put it out when the person comes?'

'I don't think so,' he said regretfully.

Again we doubled up with laughter. The incident seemed like an oasis of normality in a desert of madness. The kittens stayed there for months. They are still there now for all I know. I thought it was very considerate of him to give the dreadful ornament such a prominent place in his environment, about which he obviously cared so much, just to avoid hurting a patient's feelings.

I DREAMT ABOUT Luc one night shortly after this, something I hadn't done for a long time. In the dream I was sitting with him in his office when he left me to go into his bedroom. As he opened the bedroom door I heard a vacuum cleaner being used and knew there was someone inside. I followed him in and saw a young woman standing inside a cupboard. I sat on the bed which, unlike the double bed I had seen in reality, was a narrow single one. I exchanged a few desultory words with the woman and then Luc took me back into the office. When we got there his clothes suddenly changed; instead of his jacket and trousers he was now wearing a woman's dress, a kind of cocktail dress with padded breasts. I moved into his arms and sank my teeth into the padding. In a corner of the room there was a computer plugged into a gas pipe.

I related the dream to Luc, changing only one detail; I couldn't cope with the idea that there had been a young woman in the bedroom so I said that the woman in the cupboard was his grandmother.

'I'm telling you all this out of a kind of obligation because I know you're supposed to tell therapists your dreams. If I didn't then you could say that it's my fault that the therapy isn't working because I'm not doing what I ought to do. But it's a load of rubbish. What good does it do to have told you that?'

'What do you think the dream means?'

'Well, it's fairly obvious from the dream that I'm very curious about your bedroom and what goes on in it, but I knew that anyway. But that bit about the computer plugged into a gas pipe. What could that possibly mean?'

'What sort of things are plugged into gas pipes?'

'Cookers ... gas heaters ... so what?'

He didn't say anything. A process of Freudian association would probably have led to the conclusion that the computer represented my mother – food and warmth.

'My grandmother seems to be very important to you.'

'I reacted very strongly to your grandmother. I found her very endearing; frail and innocent. She reminded me of my mother.'

He tried to get me to talk about my parents but I was reticent. 'I don't want to talk to you about my parents. At most I'll say good things about them but nothing negative because I can't criticise them to someone like you that I don't respect. It would be showing a lack of loyalty to them.'

'Don't you think that it could be easier to talk about this kind of thing to someone you don't take seriously?'

'No.'

'Did you talk to Marion about them?'

'Yes.'

That was as far as I would go. I then had a series of dreams about him. The first one caused me to wake up screaming and I remembered just a fragment of it. I had been in his flat, in the hallway, when the young woman sprang out of a cupboard, giving me a terrible fright.

I next dreamt that I worked in the flat, as his grandmother's secretary. She was writing a book which I was typing for her on a computer which was set up in the hall. I found some half-finished knitting which I knew belonged to the younger woman and I wrenched it off the pins and unravelled it all in a fit of spiteful rage. Some time later the woman came in as I sat typing in the hallway, and I beat her up.

In another dream I was with Luc in the street, sitting on the pavement, talking as if we were in his office. He kept on talking to all the people passing by instead of to me. I pestered him constantly: 'You have to look after me. Don't talk to them. It's me you have to talk to. Listen to me.' I felt relegated to a very low rank of importance. Then we went into a restaurant where he suddenly turned into a cook and started peeling potatoes. In this dream I was very small, probably about three feet tall or less, although I still had my adult body.

We talked about these dreams, but curiously enough he didn't seem interested in going into any of it in any depth. I returned to the subject of the first dream.

'I lied to you when I said it was your grandmother in the bedroom. It wasn't her.'

'Who was it then? Your mother?'

'No, it was a much younger woman, someone of about your age.'

'Why did you lie to me about it?'

'Because I didn't want to say who it really was because I couldn't confront that.'

'I think that the person in the dream represented your mother. That's why you said that it was my grandmother. You told me that my grandmother resembles your mother. It's your mother you see in the bedroom.'

I didn't pursue this any further because I couldn't face talking about what was really intolerable to me – the fact that if there was a woman in his bedroom, she was also in his bed. I changed the subject slightly.

'The next time I come, if you're still shut up in your office with a patient when I arrive I'm going to get into your bed. I'm going to go into your bedroom, take my clothes off, get into your bed and wait for you. Then you'll come and fuck me.'

'What would you get out of that?'

'Pleasure.'

'I thought you already got a maximum of pleasure out of making love with me in your fantasies?'

'Yes, but it would be even better if you were to know that you were doing it instead of just thinking that I imagine that you're doing it.' The last sentence was nonsensical, of course, but saying this kind of thing helped to lend even more reality to my fantasies.

The next time I arrived in his flat the bedroom door was open. I noticed that there was a large mirror leaning against the wall, alongside the bed. I imagined him having sex in front of it. I thought of the other mirrors he had in the sitting room. It was like the Hall of Mirrors at Versailles. So narcissistic. And perhaps he had sex in front of the sitting room mirrors too, on the leather couches I sat on. I was trembling with rage at the idea. He was a quarter of an hour late that day and I could hardly contain the anger as I sat waiting for him.

'Why do you have all these mirrors in your flat? You're a Narcissus.' I started shouting before I'd even sat down.

There was no reply.

'And why do you have that mirror in your bedroom, opposite the bed? It's because you fuck in front of it,' I shrilled.

He was taken aback. 'What you were doing in my bedroom?' he asked aggressively.

'I wasn't in your bedroom. The door was open so I couldn't help seeing. I can't walk in holding a newspaper in front of my face like I do when I'm in the sitting room to block things out. Why don't you close your bedroom door?'

'I forgot.'

'You often forget. It's a Freudian slip. You want to display your private life to your patients. You fucking peacock! You want them to know that you fuck in front of a mirror.'

'You're jealous.'

'No, I'm not. I don't need to be jealous because I fuck with you myself. I really do. I don't just imagine it. It happens in another universe.'

'Describe this universe.'

'There's nothing in it, only me and you.'

'No gravity? No bed? No light or darkness? Neither hot nor cold?'

'No, and we don't do anything. We just have sex.'

'Am I naked?'

'Yes.'

'Do you have the same body as you do now?'

'Yes.'

'And they're bodies with pubic hair?'

'Yes.'

'Not the bodies of children?'

'No.'

As I spoke I realised that I was describing something that belonged only to the past. I no longer had these fantasies in which I had sex with him, or at least certainly not with the vivid reality that I once had. Although I still felt viscerally attracted to him I rarely now experienced the desire as something which could be gratified by normal sexual activity. I couldn't admit this to him. In fact, I didn't even want to admit it to myself. It was as if I had been defeated. By depriving me of the possibility of consummating my feelings he had managed to dominate me. I seethed with rage because I wanted to get back into my rampant sexual relationship with him, but it just wouldn't work.

The feelings I had now were much more frustrating because I couldn't even identify them. It was like having an itch which you can't quite locate – when every place you scratch turns out not to be the source of the annoyance as you had thought. I longed for him desperately and didn't know how this longing could be fulfilled. In a way it was sexual because the desire was always accompanied by a feeling of genital stimulation and a need for physical contact, but the contact I wanted wasn't a genital one. I didn't know what it was.

Whatever it was it didn't make it any easier to set myself free although rationally I saw no point in carrying on. The period of adult sexual fantasy seemed to be at an end and living through it hadn't brought about any change in me. I now seemed to be getting very heavily involved in some kind of infantile thing but I didn't see what good could come of experiencing it. It was just another weird trip. But whenever I tried to consider how I might bring things to a conclusion my mind refused to countenance the idea. My life was wholly impregnated with Luc and an independent existence was no longer possible. Not even the drugs which had given me a temporary lift could change that. In any case, the lift they had given me had been fleeting. After a few weeks they had ceased to have any effect.

At about this time I had a strange experience. I went to an evening of poetry reading to which a mother had brought a very young baby. At first I was irritated, imagining that it would spend the whole evening squalling and drowning out the poetry. It didn't. It lay contentedly in its mother's arms, quietly snorting and snuffling and feeding at the breast whenever it felt like it. I was furiously jealous. I wanted to be that baby. I *was* the baby. The baby was me and the mother was Luc. I thought about it obsessively, I rocked in his arms, I sucked his breast, and the thoughts were accompanied by very strong, almost hallucinatory, quasi-sexual feelings. I felt that if I dwelt on the idea long enough it would induce a spontaneous orgasm.

'I've something to tell you,' I told Luc.

'I'm listening.'

Unwillingly, and with a great deal of hesitation, I told him about the baby and feelings it had given rise to.

'That means you want to be my baby.'

'No!' I denied it vigorously. For some reason I hated to admit to anything of the sort. Perhaps the fact that such a desire is so obviously unrealisable prevented me from acknowledging its existence. To say yes could only lead to frustration.

Later on I lay across his knee like a baby and sucked my thumb with my legs lying across the top of the desk. I wanted to shrink till my body became short enough to be wholly enclosed in his arms. I felt that if I willed this strongly enough then it would surely happen.

I unbuttoned his shirt, right down to the bottom, exposing strong black hairs and a smooth brown stomach. I placed my head on his naked chest. Then I curled up with my thumb in my mouth.

'Why are you sucking your thumb?' he asked.

'All the better to imagine that I'm sucking your cock,' I mewled, in a childish parody of the wolf in *Little Red Riding Hood*.

I felt very contented as I lay there. I didn't need to speak.

When I finally stood up my hand brushed briefly across the front of his trousers.

'You've got an erection,' I shrieked, half horrified, half thrilled.

'Well, yes, you've been crushing my balls,' he said matter of factly.

I had just touched the end of it. It was kind of hard and soft at the same time and I didn't like it. It felt like a gigantic fat earthworm trying to rear up rigidly within the confines of his trousers. Later on in my imagination it became more like the stump left from an amputated limb. It was horrible. But it was also grotesquely fascinating. As I thought back over it I was alternately repelled by it and drawn to it. Conflicting feelings about it inhabited my mind. I wanted it sexually and was disgusted by it at the same time.

'Does that remind you of anything?' Luc asked me when I described these feelings during my next session.

'No.'

'Have you ever felt repelled by a man's penis?'

'No – at least, only occasionally. Sometimes when I'm with a lover and he wants sex and I don't and he tries to force it on me then it disgusts me. But it's nothing traumatic.'

'This feeling you had that my penis was something disgusting – don't you see that if you felt like that, then that means that you don't desire me sexually? You've regressed to a stage prior to that now. Your desire for me is something else.'

'No, that's not true. I want your body. I want sex with you.' I couldn't admit that he was perhaps right. Even though it was illogical and unsatisfactory I clung to my sexual desire for him. I didn't want to lose it; perhaps because it was something that could always be satisfied by orgasm whereas there was no possible means of satisfying all the other types of desire I was beginning to glimpse in me. Recognising their existence could only lead to frustration.

As if to bear out what I'd just said I told him about a very specific desire I'd been experiencing over the previous couple of days.

'I've been constantly haunted by fantasies in which I was sucking your penis. That was all I wanted to do with it, nothing else, and it excited me terribly. And the more I sucked the bigger it got. Just sucking it could make me have an orgasm.'

'It wasn't necessarily a penis that you were sucking. Perhaps it was a breast or a thumb.'

I looked doubtful. The question was left hanging in the air.

During this session a patient called him three times, at intervals of just a few minutes. I could hear from the timbre of the voice percolating faintly out of the phone that it was a woman, shrill and hysterical. Luc began to get exasperated.

'I've told you I can't talk to you now, I'm with a patient ... I said I'd phone you between three-thirty and four and it's only ten to four ... Well then, I'll phone you this evening. What time would you like me to call ... No, I can't talk to you now.' Finally he hung up and left the phone off the hook.

I was intrigued rather than jealous or annoyed. How many other people were there, I wondered, worked up into a frenetic state about Luc? And how many people were there in the world worked up into this kind of state about some therapist or other? It was a collective madness.

SOLIPSISM – THE doctrine that only the self is knowable. I was beginning to think that it was the least knowable thing of all. I had been plunged into a state of total confusion. All I could do was hypothesise and surmise, and no single theory about myself seemed to have any more validity than a number of other ones.

I was equally perplexed about the therapy itself. Was I undergoing a psychological mugging? Or was it a standard variant of orthodox Freudian practice, or even some original and innovative brand of treatment which I was copping out of? Was it based on sound theoretical grounds but badly handled? Was it me that just didn't know the rules of the game? Was it some gigantic bad joke which was being perpetrated on the unsuspecting neurotic? Medicalised prostitution? Emotional terrorism? Whatever the answers to these questions I felt that I was on a hiding to nothing.

For so long now I had been troubled by the arcane nature of my feelings of longing and desire for Luc – similar to sexual desire but different from it. I knew it was different because orgasm brought no relief; it didn't seem to correspond to what I wanted but I didn't know what I did want. Or rather, I did know, but it was unrealisable: constant and eternal physical and psychical communion with Luc in a universe in which only he and I existed. An impossible dream, but being brought face to face with its impossibility was shattering my psyche.

It was summer again, two years after I had gone to see Luc for the first time. On very hot days he always left the bedroom door open – to allow the air to circulate, he told me when I complained about being exposed to scenes from his personal life. One day as I passed the open door I caught sight of his easel set up just beyond where I knew the bed to be. There was a half-finished painting on it, a portrait of a young woman. I had just had a glimpse of it but I knew it to be the woman who lived there. He was painting her, in the bedroom, while she lay posing on the bed, and he cared so little about his patients' reactions that he hadn't even taken the trouble to conceal this from them. I was gnawed with anguish as I sat waiting for him, with jealousy of the woman and with anger at him for what seemed such gratuitous provocation.

I talked distractedly about something else for the first few minutes. I was too overwhelmed by my feelings to speak them. Then I got up, left the office and walked over towards the bedroom. I couldn't speak about it, but I wanted to show him that I had seen the painting. As I reached the open bedroom doorway and pointed to the easel he caught up with me and pulled me away. I broke away from him, ran into the sitting room and threw myself down on a sofa, shrieking and crying.

'You shouldn't have done it,' I screamed over and over again.

'What do you mean? What shouldn't I have done?' he asked, perplexed.

I couldn't explain. I lay face down on the sofa and sobbed, my tears dripping onto the grey leather.

'Come back into the office.' Luc held out his hand.

'Noooooooooo!'

He lifted me and half-carried me back into the other room.

'You shouldn't have done it,' I screeched again when he had settled me onto the couch. 'You shouldn't have done it. You shouldn't have let me see that you're painting that fucking bimbo who lives here in your bed.'

The look on his face began to shift from puzzlement to amusement.

'You English, you're so uncultured. That isn't a portrait of anyone here. It's a copy of a painting by Manet.'

I felt a brief surge of relief but the turmoil of my rage and jealousy kept on churning over. It was as if something had been triggered off and it was now too late to stop the process even though the original triggering factor had proved to be illusory. I was wild with rage, tears streaming down my cheeks.

'Give me a cigarette,' I demanded as he took one himself. I took the cigarette between my fingers. I hadn't smoked for four years but I needed it desperately. I put it in my mouth and I began to chew. I broke off pieces with my teeth until the whole cigarette was in my mouth. I munched. It was a bitter, acrid flavour. I looked at Luc and as I did so I knew there was a glint of madness in my eyes. I knew that I mustn't swallow. If I did, then I really would be mad.

Luc put out his hand and I spat the cigarette into it. He fetched me a glass of water. I sensed that he was troubled by what was happening. Our conversation was hesitant and unhelpful. I didn't feel better afterwards as I sometimes did when I expressed myself very violently; instead, I felt disturbed. Things were out of hand. It was crazy. It had to stop.

Shortly after this Luc went on holiday. Unlike most patients who dread their therapist's absence I had been looking forward to it as a kind of liberation. When it actually came I experienced a feeling of tremendous relief. I didn't know where he was so it was as if he didn't exist. And for fifteen days I didn't have to suffer the anguish of going to see him three times a week. I began to think about the appointment I had already fixed with him for the day following his return. Did I want to go? Would I be able to stop going? I didn't know the answers to these questions so I shelved the problem temporarily by going to London just before Luc was due back. I sent him a note cancelling the appointment, explaining that I had gone away.

I went to stay with Helen. She was in exuberant mood, in the first flush of enthusiasm of a new relationship. She advocated the same thing for me and promised to find me someone.

It was the last thing in the world I wanted. I would never have sex with a man again. Somewhere in the course of my relationship with Luc my sexual fuses had blown. I had been neutered as effectively as a spayed cat.

'Hey, what's up?' asked Helen. 'You look a bit down.' It was my first evening in London and we were drinking gin in her pine-clad kitchen.

'No, I'm fine.' I rearranged my features in the form of a smile.

'Don't look too good to me.' Helen splashed more gin into our glasses. 'Are you sure you're all right?'

What could I say? How was I going to participate in Helen's world for the next ten days? There was an awkward silence.

'Well, as a matter of fact, I seem to have cystitis. I'm feeling a bit weak.'

'Oh, you poor thing! Terribly painful, isn't it, and such a nuisance feeling you want to piss all the time and then not being able to when you try. What you have to do is slap some yoghurt up your fanny.'

'I think that's what you do for thrush.'

'Oh, yes, of course – stupid of me. Well, you'll have to go and see a quack. I'll give you the address of mine.'

To provide a cover for my strange behaviour I carried on with the charade, going to Helen's doctor with the invented symptoms and showing her the antibiotics I had been given. I spent a lot of time in bed and declined Helen's invitations to go out and meet people. I was a drag.

During this time the British hostage, John McCarthy, was released from Lebanon. There was a great deal of talk in the media about the team of psychiatrists and psychologists who would be at his disposal and about the psychological symptoms from which hostages are found to suffer, particularly during the period following their release. I envied him. A vast amount of psychiatric man-hours had obviously been devoted to this situation; extensive study had been made of the post-captivity syndrome and treatments devised for dealing with it. And yet how many hostages had there been altogether in the world? Far fewer than the victims of inept psychotherapeutic treatment, whose problems were practically ignored.

In fact, my mental state at the time was very similar to that of a released hostage. Away from Luc, with Helen in London, I was again exposed to the real world from which I had been excluded for so long. But it overwhelmed me. I was only able to communicate with people in small doses. I felt that, as far as reality was concerned, my life over the past year had been an empty hole whereas the lives of other people had been full of all the normal things.

A week later I was no less listless.

'Sure it's only cystitis?' Helen asked, with an anxiously chivvying look. 'It should have cleared up by now.'

'I don't know. I still feel out of sorts.'

'Could be M.E. You never know. Better get yourself looked at when you go back to Paris.'

'Yes, I will.'

I returned to Paris just after Luc got back. I thought vaguely that I would phone him in a day or two – or perhaps I wouldn't. Over a period of a few days it gradually became clear to me that I wasn't going to phone him. I didn't actually make a decision. It was just a state of affairs which came about in my mind.

I wanted Luc to know that I was leaving him so I sent him another note. I couldn't bring myself to address him directly so I merely copied out a sentence from a book by Maud Mannoni, a French analyst, which I thought would convey the message: *'Si l'analyste doit toujours apprendre de l'échec, il arrive alors que ce soit aux dépens du patient, ce qui n'est pas sans poser un problème éthique'*.* I hoped he would understand from it that I was no longer prepared to act as his guinea pig.

---

* If analysts are expected to learn from their mistakes this must necessarily be at the patient's expense, which leaves us with an ethical problem.

Unlike the previous occasions when I had tried to leave him, I didn't feel propelled to the phone by some unearthly force; I didn't feel frantic with grief. I was even able to think about him with equanimity and detachment. A barrier had been set up in my mind which prevented me coming into contact with anything which could make me suffer. But my life was curiously empty and no longer had any structure. Before it had been given structure and purpose by the days on which I saw Luc; the other days were just the days in between.

I spent about a week in this state.

The following week I began to feel very debilitated and depressed. I stayed in bed for several days, reading but without really seeing the words. I was physically paralysed with depression, barely able to move a limb. At times wild feelings of grief and distress would seize me and then they would diminish again to a low-level background state. It was as if I had taken an 'unhappiness drug' which caused me to drift off on a nightmare trip of generalised pain and torment without there being any concrete thing to which these feelings were associated.

I was totally isolated. I had been living a hermetically-sealed existence with Luc for a year and now it had stopped. I felt that I would never get over the experience in the same way as a parent never gets over the death of a child. It was as if I had been beaten up, pummelled into a state of physical and psychological pulp, unable to do anything other than just keep on breathing.

Then one morning I felt myself disintegrating and I knew I was going to phone him. I wasn't going to ask to see him; I just wanted to speak to him.

At the time of all my screaming I had expressed an interest in doing primal therapy and Luc had promised to get the address of a centre for me. I used this as a pretext for my call.

'I haven't got it yet,' he said.

There was a brief silence. I didn't know what to say but I couldn't bear to let him go.

'Did you get my note?' I asked.

'Yes.'

'Did you understand that it meant that I wasn't coming any more?'

'Yes.'

A dam burst inside me, a torrent of tears. I began to talk in a series of stifled squeaks. 'All the time when I've been coming to see you and it was so difficult and painful – I came just because not coming would have been even worse – but now it's changed – and now I can't come because seeing you would be even worse than not seeing you.'

'I think you should see someone,' he said. Already he seemed detached and distant, as if my problems were no longer any concern of his. I put the phone down.

The next day I phoned again.

'I want to come back.'

'Come on Tuesday afternoon at five.'

I was disturbed as I made my way to his flat. I didn't know why I was going to see him. It didn't make any sense. Then I started to be afraid. I became unbearably stressed as I sat waiting for him. When he came for me I couldn't look at him. I turned my head away. I stared resolutely at the wall, at the floor or at the window as I sat opposite him and I didn't say a word. It was as if I had been struck dumb again.

It was late afternoon, much later than I usually went. I was stiffly tense as I waited for the sound of the door opening which would tell me that the woman had come back home. It had happened once before at about this time and she had gone into the kitchen where I heard her clattering around with crockery at the other side of the wall, just a few inches from where I was sitting. I knew after the incident with the painting that I couldn't cope with it and I was afraid of what I might do. The room had one tall window. I would hurl myself against it, smashing the glass, and with such force that, even though we were only on the first floor, the impact as I hit the road below would kill me outright. Or I would hurl myself against the glass door, lacerating my whole body. Then, blood-covered, I would take up a glass shard and rip the woman to death. The potential in me for violence was boundless. And Luc wasn't in control of the situation. He had never been in control of it. He was like a child playing with a nuclear bomb.

After about fifteen minutes of this agonised anticipation I wrote a note and passed it to him. 'I shouldn't have come.'

'You shouldn't have come?' He read it aloud. 'Are you upset because I'm going to be away again next week?'

I shook my head, still without looking at him.

'Do you want to attack me?'

I shook my head again.

'Do you want me to take you in my arms?'

I shook my head, my eyes fixed on the floor. There was a strained silence for a while. Then I passed him another note. 'I want to go.'

'OK, I'll see you to the door. And I'll see you two weeks from today, at the same time.'

I shook my head but he persisted. 'I'll expect you then. Come if you want.'

I knew that I wouldn't go.

I was dazed with misery. In the days that followed I became increasingly spiritless and inert. I ate almost nothing. My stomach signalled hunger pains to my brain but my oesophagus was as if tied in knots. My body was on strike. It wanted to starve itself to death. Was I mad? And if I was, how would I know?

My mind was slowly overcome by a kind of paralysis. I carried on living mechanically.

Aftermath

A DAYDREAM haunted me repeatedly, teasing my mind, tempting me. I could go back to him and act it out if I wanted to. My mind kept on drifting off into ecstatic contemplation of the scene. I ran through the conversation we would have over and over again.

'You're going to lock the door and not let anybody else in,' I would say. 'We're going to stay here, just you and me, and you're going to look after me. And you're not going to answer the phone. You'll just let it ring. I don't want you to talk to anyone else.' Then I would scowl at him peevishly to drive the words home. He would look at me expectantly, inviting me to carry on.

'You're going to put me to bed. You're going to take my clothes off and put me into a Babygro. Do you know what a Babygro is?'

'No.'

'It's a thing for babies, like a kind of bag with bits for the arms and legs and it fastens up the back.' I curled up in a state of delicious anticipation as I thought of myself lying across his knee having the press studs done up along my spine. 'Then you're going to put me to bed and you're going to stay with me. Just you and me.' I gurgled with pleasure as he carried me into the enclosed dark warmth of the shuttered bedroom.

Later on I became obsessed with the desire for revenge. I toyed with a number of ideas. I felt destructive. I decided that I would go to his flat with a pot of gloss paint and pour it all over the furniture – the grey leather couches, the carpet, the white piano, everything. I could slip into the flat on some occasion while he was with a patient. The door was always unlocked. The more I thought about it the more determined I became to do it. But there was also something alarming about it. What if he caught me in the act? What would he do? What would I do? On one of my visits to Dr Paget for the drugs I still took I told him what I intended doing in the hope that verbalising the idea might take the pressure off me to carry it out.

'But you could end up in prison,' he expostulated, faintly scandalised.

'He wouldn't dare call the police,' I said. 'He wouldn't bloody dare!'

But it made me rethink my plans.

I finally settled on something else, something less materially damaging but more wounding. I would go to his flat with a knife and slash all the paintings in the sitting room, slash them .till the canvas was hanging in vivid, tattered ribbons. For weeks I nourished my need for vengeance with this prospect.

In the meantime my body was suffering seriously from neglect. Dr Paget directed me to a friend of his in general practice. I had blood tests done and took the results to him. He stared at them, puzzled.

'But these are the sort of results you'd expect from a Biafran refugee, or in Ethiopia. Do you eat anything?' He darted me a quizzical look over his bushy moustache.

I told him I'd been off my food because I'd been having a bad time with a psychotherapist. He grunted and wrote me a prescription for a long list of vitamins and minerals.

AUTUMN CAME. It was colder. I started to wear the clothes I had made a year previously, during the brief period when I'd been happy with Luc. I vividly remembered cutting them out in a state of reverie, tacking and stitching, the sewing machine humming and rattling in accompaniment to my thoughts of him. I wanted to go back to that period and make time stand still.

For a long time the music of Serge Gainsbourg had been intolerable to me. He had died around the time I met the woman in Luc's flat. His songs impregnated the air and became inextricably tied up with what was going on in my mind.

Then one day, early in December, I put on a Gainsbourg cassette, one with his most erotic songs; I found I was able to listen to it without being unduly disturbed.

I was out of the woods, or so I thought. Over the next few weeks I began to pick up the reins of the life I had put aside more than a year previously. My mind was no longer constantly invaded by thoughts of Luc and I found it easier to talk to people. The state of emotional mayhem I had been in had subsided to manageable proportions. At times, looking back, the whole business just seemed to be an absurdity. I started to do some forward planning.

The idea of going back to live in England appealed to me. I felt that leaving the country in which I had suffered so much would be a significant step forward to recovery. I spoke about it to Dr Paget who agreed that distancing myself from Luc in this way would be a very constructive move. Looked at from every angle it seemed the best thing to do.

I was still working in the same intermittent way for Valerie. As my state of mind improved I was able to accept more work and perform more efficiently. I now asked her about the possibility of working for her from London. She looked into the matter and agreed enthusiastically. It turned out that, even allowing for fax and modem expenses, the cost of employing me in Britain would be less than in France.

Sure, now, that I was doing the right thing, I put my flat into the hands of an estate agent and went over to London, intending to look for somewhere to live. I would have privacy this time to indulge any fits of melancholy which might still overcome me as a couple of friends had offered me the use of their house while they were on holiday.

I arrived on a Saturday evening. The grim terraced houses backing onto the railway line which carried me into Victoria were covered in a uniform layer of grey dirt. The tube stations smelt of stale soot. The area in which I was staying was not a salubrious one and the buildings had an air of seediness and neglect. Compared with Paris, London seemed to be in a state of urban blight. A germ of unease took root in me.

The following morning I went to Bethnal Green to visit a show flat in a development complex. I couldn't find it. No one I spoke to had ever heard of the place. Cold and frustrated, I decided that I didn't want to see it anyway. Retracing my steps I discovered that I couldn't find the underground station either. I was completely lost. I walked on through dismal, grimy, foreign-feeling streets until I reached St Paul's. Somewhere along the route a market was in full swing, reminiscent of the one I·used to pass on the way to Luc's, and yet so different. The Cockney cries of the costermongers, unaesthetic and barely comprehensible, repelled me. The ambience was raffish and vulgar.

By the time I got back to the house I knew beyond any doubt that I had been totally mistaken. I didn't want to be in this horrible, alien city. I didn't want to be anywhere but Paris. I ached to be back there. I found a bottle of whisky and drank myself into oblivion.

The next morning I couldn't get out of bed. The only thing which reduced the pain to bearable level was to remain curled up in a ball, knees bent up to my chin, hands gripping my upper arms, as I rocked back and forth, groaning and keening. I had ruptured the umbilical cord which bound me to Luc and I would perish if I couldn't reconnect it. I had to go back to Paris. Even if I never saw Luc again I had to be near him. I had to feel, at the very least, that I was in a relationship of physical proximity with him. And I had to surround myself with things that I associated with him; in other words, all things French.

At five o'clock I dragged myself up. I had arranged to meet Helen that evening. I went to her office. As I sat down I burst into tears. She was totally nonplussed. I mumbled some excuse about feeling unaccountably depressed and we went to a pub.

I couldn't talk to her about the one thing which preoccupied me exclusively, yet I had no energy for anything else. We made desultory conversation as we sat in the bar and then later, in a Turkish restaurant, I began to talk about Luc. I couldn't stop myself.

She listened in much the same way as one watches a horror film, both fascinated and repelled. She didn't want to hear but she wanted to know. Her eyes shifted uneasily as she asked a tentative question.

'Did you feel very dependent on him?'

'It was more than that. I was welded to him.'

I couldn't elaborate. There were no words with which to say it. Tears poured down my face. I thrust aside the kebabs and took gulp after gulp of the rough red wine.

The following day was worse. I lay huddled in a corner, unable to move, with barely the strength to cry. I called a woman I knew who worked as a therapist and told her how I felt, asking if she knew of anyone I could go and see as an emergency measure.

'If you feel that bad you should go to a hospital, to the psychiatric department. You can just walk in. I have a client who went to the Royal Free in this way and she found it very positive. Do go. You obviously need help.'

I couldn't go to the Royal Free. I was staying in NW10 and the logistics of getting to NW3 were beyond me. I looked up the telephone directory and found a hospital nearby. I rang the psychiatric department.

'You can't see anyone here,' the voice at the other end of the line told me. 'Go to casualty and they'll arrange for a psychiatrist to come over and see you there.'

The hospital was two miles away. I couldn't exercise sufficient initiative to check out the public transport, nor could I cope with the chatter of a taxi driver, so I trudged there on foot.

The waiting room of the casualty department was full of people sitting on rows of plastic chairs. None of them had any obvious injury or ailment and I wondered vaguely what could have brought them there. After two hours a young female doctor called my name. I followed her into an open plan consulting area. As she questioned me she typed my answers into a computer.

'How old are you?'

'Forty-six.'

'Have you started to have any symptoms of the menopause?'

'No.'

'Nevertheless, that could perhaps account for the way you feel.'

'I don't think so.'

She finished her questioning.

'I'd like the duty psychiatrist to have a word with you. She's busy just now, but if you'd like to wait.'

I waited for an hour and a half. Then another young woman

called my name. She took me into a small examination cubicle and we sat down together alongside the bed. As she asked me a list of routine questions she noted my answers on a standard form.

'What did your parents die of?'

'My father had cancer and my mother had a heart attack.'

'At what age did they die?'

'My father was seventy-five and my mother was seventy-eight.'

What did she think all this had to do with my present state of mind? I wondered.

'Tell me what led up to you coming here.'

I told her about the analyst. I told her that without him I was like a paraplegic. I couldn't function. I could barely breathe. And I no longer had any physical control over the expression of my feelings. I also filled her in on the plans I had for the practical changes in my life.

We had been talking for about an hour. She started to sum up, to give her diagnosis.

'I don't think you're depressed. I think you're suffering from stress. Moving house is always a stressful experience and you're not just moving house, you're moving to another country. On top of that, you've had a lot of financial problems. All these things at the same time can create a lot of stress.'

I wondered if she had paid any attention to what I'd been saying to her, or if she had any notion of what transference was like. But I didn't contradict her. She didn't seem to think that my situation merited any particular treatment so I asked her for some medication to enable me to stop crying and get out of bed in the morning. After another long wait a nurse appeared and gave me an envelope containing six small green pills. She also told me where the nearest tube station was.

I returned home by underground, slumped in a corner of the carriage. Opposite me sat a man of about thirty with sandy hair and a freckled face. He caught my eye and pulled a face, looking first lugubrious and then enquiring. I didn't respond.

'Anything wrong?' he asked, in an Irish accent. 'You look sad.'

I shook my head. But the kindly concern in his voice had made me feel even worse. My face wobbled and my eyes filled with tears. The man raised his eyebrows and cocked his head. I looked away.

The train drew into Queen's Park station. 'All change,' shouted the guard. As I stepped out onto the platform the tears flowed over. I felt the man's arm round me.

'What's wrong? Do you want to talk about it?'

He led me to a bench and sat me down.

'What is it? Has someone died?'

I shook my head.

'Trouble with your boyfriend? Husband?'

I shook my head again. There was nothing I could say. The bereavement I was suffering was infinitely worse than any of these things but I could no more communicate it than I could describe colour to a blind man. He sat with me as I sobbed. Eventually I pulled myself together and assured him that I'd be all right. We went our separate ways.

As soon as I got back home I picked up the phone and dialled Dr Paget's number in Paris.

'I need to go into a clinic,' I said, and told him what had been happening. I experienced a great gush of relief at being able to talk in French, the language in which I'd communicated with Luc and which, by virtue of this, had become my 'mother tongue' – a language of comforting, familiar and euphonious sounds.

Dr Paget agreed that I should be hospitalised and undertook to make the necessary arrangements. I called Air France and booked a flight to Paris for the next day.

The stress lessened as the plane touched down in France. I wouldn't leave after all. There could be no question of it. I didn't expect the reawakened pain to stop now that I had come back but I had learned that the suffering elsewhere would be even worse. In any case, I had no choice in the matter. 'You want to flee me,' Luc had said to me once. 'But you can't flee me.'

MY ROOM IN the clinic was small, rectangular and primrose yellow. Every morning a nurse came in and set up an intravenous transfusion. I lay immobile for an hour and a half while drugs dripped slowly into me. This method was more effective than oral administration, they said. During the rest of the day I remained almost equally immobile. There was nothing to do, nowhere to go. In any case, I didn't want to do anything or go anywhere. Sometimes I wandered round the grounds, passing other solitary, dispirited figures. Few spoke. A nightly dose of tranquillisers and sleeping pills ensured that I slept easily and deeply. I felt, in my primrose yellow cocoon, as if I was in limbo.

I became obsessed with food. The thrice daily delivery of the meal tray was the ritual occurrence which staked out the void. I checked the time constantly, counting the hours and minutes until the next tray was due. I read and reread each day's menu which was pinned up outside the kitchen. I ate everything, regardless of whether or not I liked it.

Valerie came to see me. I had had to tell her where I was as I could think of no other explanation for this prolonged absence. She was full of kindly concern but mystified. Try as I might, there was no way I could make the situation comprehensible to her.

The occasional doctor dropped in for a brief and superficial chat. Dr

Paget visited me after ten days. 'You look fifteen years younger,' he exclaimed, settling down in the yellow wicker armchair. He beamed at me, clearly pleased with the results of the treatment. The food and the artificially induced sleep had doubtless improved my appearance. Two weeks later he declared that I would soon be fit enough to go home. I didn't want to go but, seeing no constructive reason to stay, I agreed. Shortly afterwards I returned to my flat, which I had now taken off the market, and resumed life as a Parisian.

The effects of the treatment lasted no longer than my stay in the clinic. Back home I soon found myself catapulted back to my previous state. An intense feeling of grief repeatedly took me by storm, sweeping me up in waves of dizziness. And I felt that these waves were carrying me ineluctably towards death.

The feeling of grief had no identifiable object, and I therefore had nothing to mourn. I felt as I imagined I would feel if I had had a child who had died and I had subsequently lost my memory – no longer remembering the child and its death, but left still with the feelings of grief and loss in all their original intensity.

At certain times with Luc I had thought that I had reached the very acme of suffering. It wasn't so. It was even worse now. My mind had gone wild.

I thought with desperate longing about how it would have been with Luc if the woman hadn't been there in his flat. It seemed to me that it would have been like a never-ending mental orgasm. I would have felt that I was flying, free and exhilarated, like a kite on the end of a string. I had been deprived of this.

I was now even more cut off from the real world than I had been when I was still with Luc. During all that time my companion had been the radio. Even when I was incapable of giving it any attention I had it on all the time as a friendly, familiar background noise. And despite all my personal preoccupations I knew what was going on in the world. Now I didn't even have that. The great grief I felt dwarfed everything else to such an extent that nothing could be of any interest or importance. As well as that, I could neither think straight nor do anything practical. I struggled, to no avail, to change the bag in the vacuum cleaner; I could not remember which bit went where so the floors stayed dirty. The washing machine broke down; it stayed broken down. Journeys on the metro took on a random quality as I overshot my stops or drifted, unseeing, onto the wrong platforms. Tears threatened to spill forth at every turn. They were on the verge as I walked round the shelves in the supermarket, as I passed neighbours on the stair. On my occasional visits to friends I hardly dared speak for fear that opening my mouth would weaken my hold on them. My translations were shoddy, inaccurate and badly expressed. Valerie, I later found out, revised everything I did at the time.

I turned for help to the cultural centre where I had first met

Marion. It ran a weekly women's support group which I thought might provide me with an environment in which I could deal to some extent with the trauma I had been through and relearn the social skills of communicating with people. I fixed an appointment with the woman in charge of it, a cosy middle-aged American, so that we could have a preliminary talk. When I explained where I was at she seemed aghast at how much I had to unload.

'I really don't feel that the support group would be a suitable forum for you to deal with these problems,' she said worriedly. 'The others in the group would be stunned. They wouldn't be able to take it in. Their problems are more along the lines of, for example, finding it difficult to get used to working in France because their boss is rude to them. And you'd be wondering how they could be worried about such trivial things when you have all these really big issues to handle.'

I looked dejected. I didn't know where to turn.

'What I can do for you, though, is ask around and try to find a group which is working at a much deeper level than mine. There's quite a network of things going on. It's just a question of rootling about till we find something that's appropriate for you.'

I felt discouraged by this rejection. I wouldn't have minded listening to people complaining about their bosses' rudeness. I would have listened to anything provided that, in exchange, I could talk freely about what was happening to me.

A few days later she called me.

'I'm terribly sorry, but I haven't been able to find any groups which would be suitable for you. However, I've spoken to a woman who thinks she could help you. She's a hypnotherapist. I told her all about you and she'd like you to get in touch with her. She's very willing to take you on.'

'How does she work?'

'I don't really know much about it. You'll have to talk to her about that. But she claims to have a very high success rate. I think it might be worth a try.'

I was sceptical but nevertheless took a note of her number. Out of curiosity I phoned her.

'Ah yes, Lindy told me about you and I think we could perhaps do some work together.'

'I'm not sure that it's a good idea for me. What I really wanted was some kind of group therapy. I'm really scared of a one to one thing because I get so dependent on the other person.'

'My method's different. I'm not interested in getting anyone dependent on me. You do all the work yourself. I'm Californian and this is a new method which has been developed recently in California. There's a lot of work done in California which hasn't reached Europe yet. Freud's way out now. People have been doing a lot of research in California and we're just not into that Freudian stuff any more.'

'Well, what happens in your therapy?'

'I put you into a kind of a trance and you get in touch with your feelings. It's a very powerful technique. And it works very quickly. People usually just need five to ten sessions.'

'But does it involve suffering? I've done enough suffering with this man that I've been with and I can't face any more.'

'Well, it can do. Our negative feelings always involve suffering to some extent, but with the state you'll be in – this kind of trance – you'll be able to cope with it.'

'What is this trance? Is it hypnosis?'

'Not exactly, no. I don't like the word hypnosis. It's more a state of deep relaxation that I'll put you into.'

None of it was very convincing. But I was desperate. I hesitated.

'You can have a trial session free,' she said.

Against my better judgement I agreed. We arranged that I would go to her flat the next day.

A faintly disagreeable and not very intelligent-looking woman opened the door. She showed me into a sparsely furnished room with a bed along one wall.

We spoke briefly about my relationship with Luc and then she asked me to lie down, covering me with a blanket as I did so.

She began to speak.

'Relax. Let your feet go. Let them relax. Then your ankles, all the way up. Let it go. Now up to your pelvis. Let it relax. Close your eyes. How do you feel?'

'I don't feel any different.' I felt awkward and silly.

'That's because you're not giving your mind to it. You don't trust me. But that's what you came here for. You came and decided to do this of your own free will.'

'I don't believe in free will.'

'But nobody made you come here.'

I said nothing. It wasn't an appropriate setting to discuss the concept of free will.

'Let's try again. Relax your feet, then your ankles, your thighs. Relax your pelvis. Close your eyes. Concentrate on your breathing. Watch it going in and out. Now you're really relaxed and your mind's going to travel out. It's away out and it's moving towards a shining white light. Now the light's coming down to your throat. The light's in your body. It's moving down through your pelvis, into your feet and into the ground round about you.' Her voice lacked conviction and sounded slightly bored. She carried on in a monotone. 'Now your higher self is there, standing there in the light. You can speak to her.'

'I don't believe in a higher self.'

'It doesn't matter. A lot of people aren't happy with this word, but you can call it whatever you want. An inner being, God, whatever you like.'

It was beginning to sound the most terrible rubbish.

'I'm sorry, this just isn't working,' I said.

She became visibly irritated.

'Listen, we discussed this on the phone. We had a long talk about it. You agreed to come and give it a try and you're just not making any effort.'

'I'm sorry, I shouldn't have come. It's all a mistake. It's just not the right sort of thing for the problems I've got.' I began to cry. The woman looked exasperated, then her expression softened slightly.

'Listen, I think you should go to a psychotherapist. I've got an address I can give you.'

She scribbled a name on a piece of paper as I threw off the blanket and stood up.

'How much do I owe you?' I asked, thinking that perhaps the offer of a free trial session no longer stood as I had shown such a lack of cooperation.

'It's all right,' she said brusquely. She showed me to the door and we muttered an embarrassed goodbye.

Days passed, and weeks. I was in a morass of misery. At times I felt a kind of mental nausea, as if my mind was going to vomit. At others I felt that I was being sucked into death as if by a vacuum cleaner. I could no more resist it than I could resist being born.

Late one night as I walked home from the metro station I heard a child's cry. It came from the other side of the street. Looking over I saw a toddler, seemingly on its own. Some distance further on a couple loitered. They glanced back towards the child and then stood still to allow it to catch up with them. Engrossed in their conversation, they showed no interest in it. The child wailed, a plaintive and doleful sound. It teetered like a drunkard on its short little legs. The twenty yards of pavement between it and its parents seemed unbridgeable. The scene triggered something off in me in much the same way as a neurosurgeon can elicit memories or sensory perceptions by touching certain parts of the brain. I not only knew what the child felt, I felt what it felt. I was inside its mind, experiencing its distress. I had access to its consciousness and I felt anguish, outrage, affront and impotence. I walked on in a state of empathetic turmoil, wanting to put the sight and the sound behind me but unable to because they were within me. The child's pain stayed with me for days, vivid and real.

I tried once more to join a therapy group. I had recently obtained some information about a personal development centre where several different types of therapy were available. I chose a group which I thought would be suitable and contacted the woman who ran it.

134

She invited me to her flat for a preliminary discussion and we met the following day.

She said nothing once we had sat down in the small, antique-filled sitting room. I said nothing either. We stared at each other in silence and I formed a fanciful impression of her. She was like a spiritualist medium, I thought, with her long black skirt, baggy black jumper, greyish complexion and morbid expression. I visualised her, eyes half closed, in a darkened room, communing with those on the other side.

The silence continued. I thought of comparable situations, such as going to see a lawyer or any other person providing a service. They, on receiving a prospective client on their premises, would start the ball rolling. But she obviously wanted to play some kind of Freudian game, saying nothing, letting a heavy silence develop, waiting to see what would come surging out of it. It didn't seem appropriate in the circumstances. We were there to do a deal: to discuss what she had to offer and to decide whether it corresponded to my needs.

I finally gave in and started to speak, sketching out the history of my relationship with Luc. When I had finished I looked at her expectantly.

Her speech was like a series of sighs.

'These feelings of transference you talk about, that's the force you would normally work with in the relationship, the tool to be used ... ' The voice tailed off weakly. She looked as if she was in a trance.

I pursued the subject of the group. I wanted to know how it functioned and whether it could be a useful therapy for me. She was vague. I was doubtful. But in any case she had no vacancies in the immediate future, so the decision as to whether or not I should join was made for me. I was no further forward.

My need to find some means of dealing with the situation was imperative. I decided to give individual therapy one more try.

Dr Paget had at one time suggested that it might be a good idea to go to a woman as this would obviate the problem of erotic transference. He had given me a name and telephone number which I now called for an appointment.

Dr Caron's consulting room was like a boudoir. Both the room and Dr Caron herself had a slightly Viennese *fin-de-siècle* air, as if she was trying to imitate the early Freudians. She was very round, with thick black hair tied back in a chignon. The lower part of her body, with its heavy hips and thighs, resembled those fertility statues found on neolithic sites. I could easily imagine that her patients, as their relationship with her developed, would find her fascinating, mysterious and wonderfully maternal.

I told her the story of Luc and of my need for help to get over it. She suggested that I see her once a week. I hesitated.

'I'm very afraid of becoming dependent on you.'

'I'll conduct the sessions in such a way as to avoid this. I'll comment a great deal.'

I agreed to see her the following week.

During the intervening days I was increasingly overwhelmed with grief. I spent most of the time prostrate in bed, drinking myself into a state of anaesthesia.

On my second visit to Dr Caron I started to cry wretchedly as soon as I sat down, rocking backwards and forwards and howling with pain. She watched me impassively for a while and then spoke sharply. 'Stop crying.'

I gulped and sniffed.

'I have the impression that you want me to take you on my knee as that other person did.'

Nothing was further from my mind. The thought of being on her knee was even rather repellent. The inappropriateness of her suggestion sobered me down a bit.

'No, I don't want anything like that. What I want is some sort of prognosis, some idea of how long this kind of reaction is going to go on, what other reactions I can expect and when I'm going to be free of all these emotional sequels.'

'There's no prognosis.'

'In any other discipline of medicine you'd be able to give me one.'

'This isn't medicine.'

'But you're a doctor. What's the point of being a doctor in that case?'

She said nothing.

'I'd like some advice then.'

'There's no advice to give.'

'Well, perhaps some kind of drug treatment could help.'

'There are no drugs which can help you. What you feel is beyond drugs.'

'What else is there then?'

'Therapy. You need therapy to find out why you are so dependent on that man.'

I realised then that I'd had enough of therapy. I told her so and left.

Six weeks later there was a strike on the Paris metro. I had an appointment with Dr Paget at the other side of the city and only two trains out of five were running. I fretted as I stood waiting on the platform, and then lapsed into indifference as I realised that the exasperation engendered by a delayed train was of infinitesimal importance compared with the enormity of everything which had been going on in my emotional life. The train finally came and I squeezed in with a horde of angry passengers. I arrived on time.

Dr Paget was in talkative mood. He lolled back in his chair.

'To my mind it's not possible,' he said, in answer to my question about how a therapist could receive patients in his own home. 'I have a friend who's a psychoanalyst. He works at home. He had a patient who managed to lock herself up in his cellar. And then another one who came round at two o'clock in the morning, creating a scene and trying to set fire to his car. No, no, it's just not possible.' He shook his head.

I was reassured to hear about all this excessive behaviour. It made me feel that I wasn't unique, that my feelings were simply a manifestation of a syndrome.

I took my prescription and walked back to the metro station. The ticket window was closed. A notice informed passengers that there would be no more trains that day. I was four miles from home.

I started to walk. It was late in the day and it was cold. I trudged down the Champs Elysées, continually checking the road for a taxi. They were all full. I carried on. It started to rain and I had no umbrella. The streets were thronged with pedestrians deprived of transport and there was an unwonted air of camaraderie. I reached the Seine after about half an hour. As I walked over the Ile de la Cité I realised that I was getting dangerously close to Luc's flat. I would have to make a wide detour to avoid it. Since I had known Luc the whole of central Paris had been as if radioactive.

Once I reached the Left Bank, however, I carried straight on. I was tired, wet and cold. I wasn't going to prolong my journey. And in any case, now that I was so near, I felt drawn to the flat, like a moth to a candle flame. I was terrified that he would see me and think that I was prowling round the neighbourhood in the hope of seeing him, but I would just scuttle quickly past, taking only a furtive glance.

My mind broke out in gooseflesh as I approached. My legs wobbled. I rounded the corner leading to his street and looked fearfully up. The whole flat was in darkness and the shutters swung forlornly in the wind. A large notice was displayed in the sitting room window. 'To let,' it said. He had gone. He no longer lived there.

I knew at once what I was going to do. I memorised the estate agent's number and the next day I called it.

'I see you have a flat in the rue X,' I said in reply to the brisk male voice which answered the phone. 'I'm looking for something in that area. Could you tell me about it, please.' He described the flat and told me the rent. I said I would be interested in seeing it. We made an appointment for the next day.

I felt a terrible dread. I was going to walk back into that flat, not only into the rooms I had already seen, but also into the inner sanctum, the areas which had always remained hidden. I would be reliving the most intimate and the most painful experiences of my life, and I would be doing so in the company of a salesman under the impression that we were there to negotiate a lease.

An ebullient man in a smart grey suit greeted me outside Luc's flat.

'Madame Alexander?'

'Yes.'

I squirmed under his appraising look. I was sure that I didn't look like the sort of person who could afford a flat of this standing and that I had already been marked down as a time waster.

He took a set of keys out of his pocket and opened the maroon door. I followed him in.

We crossed the hallway and passed into the irregularly-shaped sitting room. Emptied of its furniture it seemed oddly cavernous. I paid scant attention to the estate agent as he enumerated the qualities of the flat. This was the room in which I had waited for Luc on countless occasions, tense, anguished, stressed, full of frustrated longing. These feelings assailed me again.

'A very good-sized room,' the estate agent concluded.

We moved on to the bedroom.

I had only seen half of the room before, the view from the threshold as I talked to Luc's grandmother, the gaudy bedspread, and then, later, the unfinished oil painting. I now stood in the middle of it. I looked at the empty space where the bed had once stood and visualised what Luc used to do there. I saw heaving buttocks and entangled limbs and seethed with jealous rage. The estate agent continued his sales talk.

'There's also a smaller bedroom,' he said. 'If you would just follow me, please.'

We went into the room where Luc had received his patients. Without the blue velvet couch running along one wall the proportions were transformed. I felt disorientated. The idea that someone else was going to move into the flat and use the room for some banal purpose – sleeping, or office work perhaps – was inconceivable. I couldn't reconcile my experience with such notions. This room was the epicentre of the earthquake which had shattered my life.

The estate agent gave me a sideways look. Had he asked me a question, perhaps, one to which I had made no reply? I had no idea what he'd been saying.

'I'll show you the kitchen and bathroom now,' he said.

We went down the corridor along which I had often inquisitively peered and turned left into the kitchen. I was suprised to find myself in a kitchen just like any other. It was difficult to imagine Luc in such a mundane environment. It diminished him.

'Big enough to eat in,' said the estate agent.

We crossed over to the bathroom. I felt uncomfortably voyeuristic as I stood between the bath and the washbasin and thought of all the things Luc used to do there, intimate things associated with his body. I didn't like being there. I wished I hadn't come. I wanted to flee.

'I think we've seen everything, then,' the estate agent said. 'What do you think?'

I groped around in my mind for something appropriate to say. The estate agent looked at me enquiringly.

'It's a very nice flat,' I stammered. 'But I'm not sure. It's rather more than I wanted to pay.'

'Come now,' he said reprovingly. 'In an area like this what do you expect?'

I said nothing. We went down the stairs and shook hands in the street.

'Thank you very much,' I said. 'I'll let you know.'

I walked back past the window of what had once been Luc's consulting room.

'*Côtes de porc,*' roared the red-faced butcher standing under it in the doorway of his shop, legs splayed and arms akimbo, his apron stained with blood. He had no idea of what used to go on just above his head. I almost smiled, but then, as I walked on, I was overwhelmed by a feeling of ineffable sadness.

Epilogue

IT IS NOW over three years since I last saw Luc. As with any other bereavement, the pain diminished over a period of time. Instrumental in my making a quantum leap forward was my discovery of a London-based support network for people who had had negative experiences of therapy. There, for the first time, when I spoke with its founders, Vera and Carol, I felt that I was talking to people who not only understood but were able to take on board what I was saying. My dialogue with them was very different from the Alice in Wonderland type of exchanges I had been having with practitioners thus far. As I spoke I had the impression that they were on familiar territory. They had heard it all, or things very similar, before.

'You're in a state of shock,' said Vera. It was comforting, somehow, to hear this after being told so often and so peremptorily that my feelings were a manifestation of deep-seated emotional problems that could only be resolved by more and yet more therapy. Shock, I felt, was something that I might reasonably expect to evaporate, eventually, of its own accord.

Even their admissions of ignorance were reassuring after so much glibly claimed expertise.

'Why?' I asked. 'Why do I feel like this?'

'We don't know,' said Carol quietly. 'As far as this sort of thing is concerned we're just emerging from the primeval swamp.'

I was later able to leave Paris and move to London. This time there was no irresistible gravitational force to be fought against and I implemented the plan previously arranged with Valerie which enabled me to continue working for her.

I made contact with other members of the network and heard my experiences echoed in those of people who had suffered in similar ways. I felt a terrific sense of deliverance when I realised that I was no longer alone, no longer a unique being from another universe.

Jane talked compulsively about a therapy which she had undergone ten years previously. She still felt disorientated, traumatised, psychologically disturbed.

Thomas had been trapped for twenty-three years, unable to leave therapy but so undermined by it that he had never been able to establish a relationship with a woman.

Margo had been in therapy with a pupil of Wilhelm Steckel, a close associate of Freud. Now, fifty years later and aged over eighty, she still talked eloquently of the damage done to herself and the disastrous consequences on her marriage and children.

Maureen's therapy with a woman who, she felt, was more than life itself to her, had ended abruptly when the therapist informed her at the beginning of one session that it was to be her last. Every day for the next six months Maureen had bought a bunch of flowers and laid it on her therapist's doorstep at her usual appointment time. 'Like laying a wreath on a grave,' she said, still melancholy after more than a year.

Not much needed to be said for empathy to be established, we were so tuned in to the state of mind which can be engendered in therapy. We were part of a kind of freemasonry of people who had experienced things others could barely imagine.

'How did it affect your relationships with other people?' I asked Christie.

I was curious about Christie. She was vivacious, attractive and articulate. Surely she had sufficient psychological cushioning to be able to withstand a bad time at the hands of an inept or misguided therapist?

'What other people?' she asked, amusedly scornful, as if to say, 'You should know better than to ask that question.'

I did indeed know. When you are transported into the other world of transference there *are* no other people. On good days the rest of your life – family, friends, work, domestic and other concerns – is on the back-burner. On bad days it simply doesn't exist.

Surely, though, this couldn't apply to someone like Christie.

'But you strike me as such a dynamic and resilient person,' I said to her. 'How could a therapist have affected you so much?'

'I guess no one's immune.' She rolled her eyes. 'The dark forces of the subconscious!'

These forces were such that they had almost driven her to lie down on the road with her head under the wheels of an oncoming bus, she told me later. It was at a time when her therapy seemed to have generated a state of profound despair. Walking down the King's Road she felt an overpowering urge to have herself killed by each red double-decker bus that she saw approaching. Panic-stricken, feeling her will to resist disintegrate, she jumped into a taxi and had herself taken to a hospital casualty department.

'They'd no idea what I was talking about. There was this young doctor – about twenty-eight I think – and he said to me, 'The world is a nice place to be in. There are lovely things in it. What do you want to do away with yourself for?' He hadn't a clue. There was nothing he could do for me. But at least it got me away from the buses on the King's Road for a bit.'

Epilogue

'IF DANTE HAD known about psychotherapy he would have had a special circle in hell where people would be afflicted with unresolved transference,' said Sylvia wryly. She was a delicate but cosy woman of about fifty with a childlike air, reminiscent of a Degas ballet dancer. Not an image that I could easily reconcile with the extreme and bizarre emotions under discussion.

Yet most of Sylvia's adult life had been spent in the throes of dependency on one therapist or another. All her material and social needs had been subordinated to the psychological imperative of maintaining these relationships. A graduate in fine art, she had worked for twenty years as a copy typist, doing shift work so that she could arrange her hours around her therapy appointments. These were so costly in relation to her typist's wage that she had to temp on her days off in order to pay for them. Even so, working sometimes fifty hours a week, her therapy fees left her with barely enough to survive and she was obliged to live in almost slum conditions.

She shuddered as she looked back to that time. We were sitting in the kitchen of a little attic flat in Clapham which she had since been able to buy with an inheritance.

'Oh, it's all coming back to me now. I haven't thought about that period for ages. Suppressed it, I suppose, it was so ghastly.' She laughed in her dulcet fashion as she filled the kettle.

'What was it like, this place that you say was so grotty? I can't imagine you living in squalor.'

'Oh, it was simply dreadful. I had two rooms – two tiny little rooms – and I shared the bathroom with seven other people. It was so filthy that sometimes I would have to wait till I got to work to go to the toilet. And I could never use the bath, of course, it was so disgusting. No-one ever cleaned it. The rent was cheap because everything was so awful and also because the arrangement with the landlord was that if anything needed done in the way of decoration and so on, we would do it. But no one ever did. The place just went to rack and ruin. Peeling walls, rotting woodwork, ugh!'

'What about the other tenants? Did you get on with them?'

'Oh no, they were all really weird. And so noisy. That was one of the worst things. There was a blind man above me who played jazz in a club and he used to come home at one in the morning, drunk, and start to play his drums, really loudly, almost every night. I could never get to sleep.'

'Didn't you speak to him about it.'

'I did once, but he threatened me. I didn't dare mention it again. Then there was a man next door who was deaf. He used to have the television blaring all evening. And in the afternoon there was a girl underneath who played country and western music for hours on end, always the same song, over and over again. It was like the Chinese water torture.'

It sounded like another special circle for Dante's hell.

'What did your parents think of you living in a place like that?'

'They didn't know. Oh, gosh, no! I never let them come there. They'd have been horrified.' She was rummaging around in a cup-board. 'Earl Grey or Darjeeling?'

'I don't mind.'

'Earl Grey then, I think.' She spooned the tea into a pot.

'George didn't know about any of this, though,' Sylvia continued. George had been her therapist at the time. 'He couldn't have imag-ined it, anyway. He'd no idea how people without money lived. He'd no idea how materially deprived I was on account of the therapy. Not that it would have made any difference even if he had. I asked him once if he would still see me if I couldn't pay, if I'd no money, and he said, 'Well, I wouldn't lose all interest in you, but I wouldn't see you, oh no.' And the funny thing is, I didn't mind paying him. He used to leave his bill on the pillow of the couch, once a week, and I used to think of it as a kind of *billet doux*. I used to treasure them like love letters even when I didn't know how I was going to pay them.'

'What about your social life?' I asked.

'I didn't have one. I'd no money, of course, to do anything – to go to the cinema or a restaurant or anything like that. And anyway all my mental energy was absorbed by the therapy. My whole life revolved around the sessions. My whole being was devoted to the relationship with George. I pined for him all the time, you know. The only time I didn't pine for him was during the sessions. Week-ends were particularly difficult. And the holidays! Oh, dear!' She laughed self-deprecatingly. 'You see, what made it so difficult was that I had no sense of identity apart from him. When he was away on holiday I didn't know who I was. He was the ground I walked on. He made my body solid.' She was beginning to look profoundly serious. 'Then, after I'd been with him for nine years, he died.'

The kettle began to whistle. Sylvia added the boiling water to the tea and left it to infuse, muffled snugly in a rabbit-shaped cosy.

'Yes, it was on New Year's Day. His son phoned me. He said, "This is George Grant's son. I have some very bad news about my father. He died last Thursday." Just like that.' She stopped, as if for a minute's silence in remembrance.

'What did you do?' I asked. The question sounded banal and inadequate.

'Well, he gave me a number to call. I dialled it right away and the person – she was a therapist from George's professional associa-tion – said, "You're going through a bereavement, and bereavement is a growing process." As if it was all part of my therapy! As if I ought to be grateful for this stepping-stone which was going to help me move on towards greater emotional well-being!' Sylvia looked bemused, still aghast at the memory of such lack of understanding. She poured the tea and offered me a garibaldi biscuit.

'It didn't, of course. Move me on, I mean. And there didn't seem to be any structure for dealing with the situation. The association didn't have any kind of support to make available. They get you into this situation of total dependency and then leave you with no resources when you suddenly find yourself bereft of the person you've been dependent on. The only thing that held me together was Sister Agnes. She was a nun I knew. I remember thinking, as I stood on the edge of the platform at Finsbury Park tube, wanting to throw myself under the train, "Sister Agnes, I'll go to Sister Agnes". So I went. And I stayed in the convent for six weeks, being looked after. It was the only thing I could have done. Otherwise I just wouldn't have survived.' She stirred her tea slowly.

'And then – oh, it was absolutely awful – I was invited to a memorial concert for George, not so very long after he died. It was like a wake, with everybody looking jolly. His family were there looking jolly and bright, and they played George's favourite music. The place was full and there was this sea of smiling faces. And dotted about here and there among the smiles were those agonised faces. And you knew – those ones were his patients. It was so cruel.'

'How did you eventually get over it?'

'I got another analyst. I went to a therapy centre and asked them to give me somebody. They tried to tell me that it was best just to mourn George for a while, without having recourse to anyone else, but I told them I couldn't. There was no way I could even breathe at the time without an analyst. So they put me on to Dr Harris. But that's another story!' Sylvia laughed. 'That one will really make your hair stand on end. But I'll tell you about it some other time. Enough of all this analyst talk!'

We finished our tea and went out to the theatre.

After the play we resumed our 'analyst talk' over a couple of capuccinos in a pizzeria.

'This business about the dependence,' said Sylvia, 'it doesn't seem to matter whether the therapist encourages it or discourages it. It's just there, like the weather. I had a friend who only went to her therapist once a month but she was totally obsessed with him. She thought about him morning, noon and night. And it's so invasive, so overwhelming. I met her walking down Harley Street once in floods of tears – in public! – because she was so distressed about something that had happened during her session.'

It was a relief to me to hear this. I had always been uncomfortable with the memory of crying in the tube train, making such a spectacle of myself in front of the unknown Irish man, but it now seemed that I wasn't the only one.

'And I think that very often even the therapists themselves don't

understand strong transference,' Sylvia continued. 'Just imagine –
Clare, my first therapist, used to encourage her patients to paint,
and she used to put their paintings on the wall. And she expected
me to take an interest in these paintings and chat about them, when
all the time it made me so angry and jealous. She didn't seem to
have a clue about how it was making me feel.'

'If that had been me she wouldn't have been in any doubt about
how it was making me feel,' I said. 'I'd have ripped them off the
wall. I'd have spat on them and thrown them out the window.'

A solitary man at the next table looked askance at us as he
twirled spaghetti round his fork.

'Yes, but we're very different,' said Sylvia. 'Funny, isn't it, that
we're so different but both so susceptible to being dependent. Why
do you think that is?'

'God knows,' I said. 'Or perhaps He doesn't. Do you think anyone
knows?'

Sylvia shrugged.

'Do you think it did you any good?' I asked. 'Did you get anything out of it at all?'

Sylvia toyed with a sugar cube as she considered the question.

'Well, I did feel slightly less depressed after nine years with
George, and I did feel slightly less dependent at the end of the
twenty years, but who's to say that I wouldn't have experienced the
same differences without therapy? People often have emotional problems when they're young, and then start to feel more stable when
they're in their thirties. I've no idea how things would have been
otherwise. I might have got married, had children, had a proper
career. These things might have brought a whole different set of
problems with them, of course. Who knows? As regards the efficacy
of therapy in general, I suppose I have to remain agnostic, but all I
can say is that it's no way to spend a life.'

ALICE WAS AN artist. The walls of her sitting room were lined with
paintings which were curiously hybrid in style. Viewing from a distance, one had the impression of bare landscapes – desert, arctic,
wilderness. But studied more closely, they transformed themselves
into compositions of striking intimacy, patterns of human figures
twined together in delicate and expressive embrace.

'Why do you have this amalgam of animate and inanimate?' I
asked. 'I'm afraid I'm a bit of a philistine but I don't see the
relationship between the two.'

'It's all to do with the superficial and the profound,' said Alice.
'And also the actual and the potential. The arid and cold exterior
contrasted with what we feel underneath. Now this one, you see,'
she pointed to a couple of stunted, curiously humanoid growths, like

leafless bonsai trees, which wrapped their bare branches clumsily but lovingly round each other. 'We are so warped, but we still have this tremendous capacity to love, to cherish. It's just not nourished enough. It somehow doesn't manage to flourish as it should.' There was a note of exasperated frustration in her voice.

Alice was sixty but looked younger, despite years of grief and torment spent with a therapist who sounded like a past master in the art of emotional torture.

'What's so amazing is that I found myself having therapy without realising what was going on, like drinking a ... what is it you call it? When someone slips a drug into your drink because they want to rob you or rape you or something?'

'A Mickey Finn.'

'Yes, that's right. A Mickey Finn. That's just what it was like. I'd taken my daughter to this man for child guidance, you see. She'd been quite disturbed after my husband and I split up. And he started analysing me without telling me what he was doing. We just used to have these sessions, about the family situation. And before I knew it I was addicted. I was in a fully-fledged state of transference.'

'Didn't you think this was a bit dubious?'

'Well, no. He was a medical doctor as well as an analyst, and very experienced, with all sorts of letters after his name. Anyway, I became totally dependent very quickly and I was in such pain all the time, emotional pain. It was as if he was stirring things up in me. I just went about all the time with these pains and the frightful suffering. Great waves of pain used to break in on me like an evil force. But I couldn't leave him any more than a child could leave its mother. I had to keep on going back to get those pains healed, but they never did get healed. It just seemed to get worse and worse. He always seemed to say the wrong thing, react in the wrong way, so the suffering just increased. And of course, it had a terribly damaging effect on my social life. I couldn't ever make any plans to do anything, for example, because I never knew how I would be feeling. I just couldn't function socially.'

'How did it affect your relationship with your daughter?'

'Well, that's about the one thing that I could still cope with. As far as she was concerned I was always able to hold together.'

'I just asked because I've been reading *One to One*.* Do you know it? A book in which a number of people describe their experiences of therapy. Anyway, one of these people, Harriet, said that sometimes when her children were sick, she had to cancel her appointment, and she practically hated them for it. And she said that that was what she resented most in the end, the fact that her children's lives had been so blighted by the whole business.'

'Yes, I can understand that. I can see how it could quite easily

---

* Rosemary Dinnage (1988), *One to One*. London: Penguin.

happen. But, as I say, I did just about manage to provide a stable relationship for my daughter, though really, it was a miracle.'

'Did you feel sexually attracted to the analyst?'

'There may have been an element of that but it wasn't very dominant. Except on one occasion. Oh, it was dreadful. I'd had a dream about being adolescent and I told him about it. He started talking about the bodily changes that a girl goes through at puberty, about breasts and vagina and pubic hair and all that. I felt all of a sudden as if I'd been given an aphrodisiac. I was simply overwhelmed with sexual desire, not just for him, but for anyone who looked like him. On the way home I felt a kind of compulsion to throw myself at every oldish, grey-haired man that I saw; to rip my clothes off, like a nymphomaniac. I was in such a state of distress during the weekend, tormented with sexual desire and feeling that I wasn't going to be able to control myself, that I had to phone my GP. He had to come round and give me emergency sedative treatment. I was utterly humiliated.'

'How long did you spend with this analyst?'

'Sixteen years.'

'Then what happened?'

'He was quite old. He said he'd be retiring soon. Then he said he'd need a break for a bit so I didn't see him for a few weeks. Then he wrote to me and said that he wouldn't be able to see me any more. That was all.' A fleeting look of outrage passed over Alice's face.

'I tried to get help from another analyst I'd known but she just said, "I think you ought to take responsibility for your life yourself now." As if I could! I suppose I had a total breakdown after that. I just collapsed. I had a friend who was a therapist and she understood. She took me into her home and looked after me. I was helpless, like a baby. I just cried all the time. I couldn't bear to be alone, not for a minute. Sometimes she even took me into bed with her, just to hold me, to comfort me.'

My eyes fell on the painting behind her, a sandstorm from the whorls of which emerged a shape reminiscent of an adult carrying a child, enclosing it tenderly in its arms.

'I was in such a broken down condition,' Alice continued. 'Then after a while I felt I couldn't stay with her any longer, it wasn't fair. I got medical help and it was arranged that I would attend a day hospital. An ambulance came for me every day. I'd have been quite incapable of getting there myself, I was so undermined with depression.'

'What was it like in the day hospital?'

'Oh, everyone was very depressed. I was surrounded by all these depressed people. We used to play games. Trivial Pursuit, things like that. And drink endless cups of tea. That was all really. And I was on drugs, of course. I attended the day hospital for four months.'

'Sounds pretty grim. But at least you had Trivial Pursuit. In the place I was in you were left to your own devices all day long. Anyway, how did you manage to escape from all that?'

'Well, I simply had to find another therapist. There really wasn't any other solution. My therapist friend – the one who took me in – found me someone, the man I go to now. Yes, I feel much better now. I like the way it's progressing. I'm still very dependent but he seems to be able to contain it. It's not so invasive. But on the other hand, I can't ever see myself being able to do without it.'

I noticed a cloudscape, billowing shades of white revealing a child nestling papoose-like against an adult back.

'Why is this one better?', I asked. 'I mean, what do you think is the difference between a good therapist and a bad one?'

'Well, I can't generalise. But if I think about my own experience, and also other people that I've talked to, I think perhaps it all depends on the bond between therapist and patient – on their particular relationship, not on any particular theory. Like marriage.'

TALKING WITH MAUREEN one day, I gained a new angle on what may have been happening to me the morning I woke up unable to open my eyes and feeling as if I was being injected with anaesthetic, with head swimming and limbs like cotton wool. Maureen described something very similar.

'I'd been feeling very peculiar for a couple of days, as if my body was being rubbed, and at the same time I felt a tremendous love for my therapist, even more than usual. Then the next day I had the most terrible headache. I felt very ill and frightened. And I was blacking out constantly, as if I was being pushed down into a very black hole. I staggered to the phone and called my therapist. She said, 'It's all right, I am here.' I was very reassured and the next time I saw her she said, "Well, we've got to look after this baby, haven't we?" I felt totally good afterwards but very, very weak. And I've felt ever since that I know exactly how babies feel, and how important their birth is.'

I had had a vague notion at the time that some of my own experiences in therapy had something to do with birth, but birth in reverse, as if I had my own personal arrow of time which was travelling backwards, bearing me towards the pre-conceptual void. But perhaps it had been, as Maureen believed, a reliving of the actual birth itself. This would tie in with a number of the other psychic phenomena that I had experienced which could be identified with situations at or before birth. The feeling of being welded to Luc, bound together in a state of ecstatic communion with him, unable to have any separate existence. The feeling of being in another universe with him, a universe occupied by him and me alone. The need to seek out enclosed, cocoon-like places. The fantasy that my bed was an incubator. The fantasy of being cut away from a Siamese twin, leaving the other with all the vital organs, source of nourishment and life. Most of all, the answer that came to me so strongly and surely as I wondered what it would have been like if I had never discovered the woman in Luc's life – that it would have been like flying, free and exhilarated, like a kite on the end of a string. I have no difficulty in associating this image with that of an embryo floating on the end of the umbilical cord in the amniotic fluid.

But so what? *'Et alors?'* I would have said to Luc.

My feelings for Luc when I was still with him were so intense that I was quite unable to attempt any objective analysis, trying to connect them to likely events in my childhood or to my relationships with my parents. Even now, although able to examine them more dispassionately, I can see no links. Contrary to what one might suppose from my behaviour with Luc, I have no younger brother or sister; there was no later pregnancy to threaten my relationship with my mother. Nor could I make any sense of the sexual desire I felt for this person (incorporated in Luc) who was male one minute, female the next, and shared no discernible characteristics with any of the significant personae in my life. I can make neither head nor tail of the whole thing. And if I could, would that move me any closer towards my original goal of acceptably assertive behaviour? Would it make me less anxious, less guilt-ridden, more self-confident, more balanced? I think not. And even if it did, would it justify such colossal emotional expense? Again, I think not.

I VISITED MARGO recently. She is eighty-four and still remembers every vivid detail of her therapy but talks mostly of other things.

We discussed the disintegration of the health service over lunch.

'All part of the disastrous heritage of that Thatcher woman,' said Margo, 'the architect of Britain's decline.'

Afterwards we sauntered round the shops. Margo wanted to show me the 'in' places to buy clothes. I watched as she muscled in alongside teenagers in Mark One, searching the rails for a waistcoat to go with her elephant cord trousers. She found one to her liking and tried it on.

'How do I look?' she asked, tugging it straight and scanning herself in the mirror.

'The height of fashion,' I assured her. 'Very chic.'

We walked down the lane to her house. Margo stopped in front of a bush to admire an exceptionally large spider's web.

'Just look at this. Now, wouldn't you call that a miracle? How do they do it, I wonder. How do they manage to weave all this without any support?'

I bent down. It was an orb web. 'I think they start off with a bridge line. Then they construct a kind of framework. But this is quite a simple one. D'you know, there's something called a bowl-and-doily spider, which gets its name from the shape of its web. You can imagine what that's like. Then there's the bolas spider which doesn't spin a web at all. It just shoots out a line of silk with a sticky blob on the end and swipes its prey that way.'

'Amazing,' said Margo. 'Nature is such a treasure chest of fascinating facts, isn't it?'

Back in her house Margo put on some jazz and made tea.

'Tell me, dear,' she said when we were sitting down, 'how do you feel about your therapist now? What is it – three years since you left him?'

'Well, obviously I feel much better. In fact, I suppose there's no pain any more. But, funnily enough, I still want to die. I don't mean I feel suicidal. I'm not going to kill myself, no fear of that. It's just that I kind of look forward to dying. Not just dying, but being annihilated. Yes, that's it. I look forward to being totally annihilated, not existing any more. That way I won't have even the memory of that dreadful suffering. And also because everything seems to have been diminished. Nothing could really matter all that much after what I experienced then.'

Margo looked at me sceptically. 'Oh, come on. Somebody who's interested in spiders' webs doesn't want to be annihilated.'

There was some truth in what she said. It was the 'Schopenhauer's tangent' effect again. But I felt that some of my truth lay also with Harriet of *One to One* who finished her account thus:

I suppose I sort of recovered. And yet I haven't. ... I don't think you recover that much from an actual smashing up of yourself, when everything is turned upside down and in a way you stay sane but underneath things are quite weird and mad. In a way you're always in a dream for ever after.

Afterword

ERNESTO SPINELLI

I SUSPECT THAT most readers who have read through Ms Alexander's account of her therapeutic odyssey will have been substantially disturbed by it. I suspect, as well, that those readers who also happen to be practising psychotherapists will have experienced the kind of shock that only arises when a particularly powerful truth – no matter how unpalatable – presents itself in such a way that it cannot be avoided nor denied any longer.

Ms Alexander was undoubtedly a difficult client. She herself admits this. However, it would be all too easy – and unfair – to focus upon this aspect of her account in order to explain or assuage the injustices she suffered in the name of therapy. Nevertheless, it would not be surprising to find some therapists insisting upon an extensive focus of Ms Alexander's character and the snippets of her history as revealed throughout the text as a means to circumvent the impact of the issues with which she confronts us. Indeed, some therapists might argue that unless and until far greater knowledge of Ms Alexander's personal history and background were made available, no suitable judgement of her therapeutic experience could be made. While some readers might be in partial agreement with this viewpoint, at least insofar as they might have wished to know more of her previous experiences and relations with others, I am personally of the opinion that such factors are largely irrelevant to the principal concerns that the account raises. Since Freud, and the impact of his ideas upon Western culture, we have tended to assume that biographical material is essential to the proper understanding of expressed views and opinions. More than that, some therapists have employed aspects of their clients' biographies as a means of explaining – or excusing – their (that is, the therapists') misuses and abuses of power and authority. This tendency, sadly, has been most apparent in the defence of psychoanalytic theories and practices when they have been criticised or attacked. For instance, when presented with the need to respond to Jeffrey Masson's devastating critiques of psychoanalysis, many analysts chose to focus upon what they interpreted as being serious flaws in his personality rather than address and criticise the issues under question (Masson, 1992).

More recently, Frederick Crews's critiques have been dealt with in the same fashion by some 'defenders of the faith' (Crews, 1995). Such *ad hominem* arguments strike me as being deeply repugnant and are a far cry from the avowed scientific aspirations of psychoanalytic theories. I raise this issue at the outset because it would not be surprising to find that similar strategies may well be employed by some in response to Ms Alexander's testament to the failure of her therapy.

Actually, it would be more accurate to say 'therapies' since her account presents us with nearly a dozen meetings of varying length with a variety of psychiatrists, psychoanalysts and psychotherapists. Each of these, in his or her own way, while clearly seeking to assist Ms Alexander in dealing with her problems, also manages – however inadvertently – to provide her with novel ones which, in several cases, overwhelm (if not overthrow) the initial presenting issues. While it is not unusual (though by no means inevitable), particularly in the early stages of therapy, for some clients to uncover previously unconsidered problematic concerns in their lives, many of the hindrances that Ms Alexander faces arise directly out of her contact and meetings with her therapists and are specific to the therapeutic interventions that are provided. While it would be fair to acknowledge that one's relationship with one's therapist might express in a specific or microcosmic fashion more general, or macrocosmic, difficulties in one's self/other relations, it is quite another matter when the therapeutic relationship that is engendered itself becomes a – if not the – problem.

For instance, both Dr Weissmann and Dr Landau instigate negative responses from Ms Alexander when, in the course of their meetings, they allow themselves to 'take time out' to answer their telephones and engage in conversation with their callers during Ms Alexander's session time. I find such behaviour to be both unprofessional and inexcusable. While there may be extenuating circumstances whereby a personal urgency might require a therapist to interrupt a session, one would expect therapists to warn their clients of such possibilities at the start of a session and, even then, an apology for such an interruption would be expected. Neither therapist, however, seems to even consider this, nor does either see fit to clarify what the experience and meaning of these intrusions might be to Ms Alexander and to her perception of the relationship that exists between them. Rather, it appears implicit in Ms Alexander's account that each views her outbursts of anger or discomfort as having little to do with *their* behaviour and, rather, interprets such as unjustified expressions of *her* 'neurosis'.

In the same way, when Dr Weissmann ends his thirty-minute session five minutes early so that he can be on time to catch a train, he does not seem to deem it important enough to mention this change in their contract until the moment when he announces that the session is over. Indeed, Dr Weissmann appears to work under the principle that it is he – and he alone – who is in the position to decide the length of an individual session. Just as, in a similar fashion, it seems that it is solely up to him to determine whether he wishes to arrange a second session with Ms Alexander so that *he* can decide whether or not to continue working with her. That Ms Alexander might wish or be able to make her own decision on this matter does not appear to be a matter worthy of his consideration.

And again, when Ms Alexander asks Dr Weissmann if he likes her, his initial response is to murmur 'Mmm, I'm not sure,' (p. 11) and, in the following session to drawl 'I think, after all, I find you quite likeable ... Because of your intelligence. And there's something a bit wild about you that appeals to me .... You're a rum character' (p. 11). What is one to make of this arrogant nonsense masquerading as candour? Ms Alexander's last words to Dr Weissmann seem pertinent here: 'I need to know why you played it the way you did. I want you to explain this to me. It's the only thing that can help' (p. 17). But, unsurprisingly, Dr Weissmann is unable, or unwilling, to offer a reply that directly addresses their relationship and, instead, employs her request as a means to reassert his view of Ms Alexander's psychic 'fragility' (p. 17).

If Dr Weissmann presents us with a near-parody of therapy in its most disagreeable aspects, Dr Luc Landau's therapeutic relationship with Ms Alexander comes close to tragedy. Initially experienced by Ms Alexander as being caring, attentive, easy to talk with, and willing to listen to and consider her requests and criticisms of him in a direct and open fashion, unfortunately he, too, either provokes or exacerbates Ms Alexander's downward spiral towards misery and confusion both with regard to herself and to her relationship with him. While many of the problems that ensue are likely to have been either inadvertent or, paradoxically, arose out of Dr Landau's well-intentioned desire to assist his client, their seriousness is indisputable. As I see it, many of these are the result of his giving his client either incomplete or mixed messages. For instance, while some therapists would see it as problematic, I do not personally take issue with Dr Landau's suggestion to Ms Alexander that she can write to him while she is in Africa. What *is* problematic, I believe, is that he does not make the 'ground rules' specific in that he does not clarify that he, in turn, should not be expected to respond to her letters. That he does not make this proviso plain only succeeds in provoking his client's confusion and anger and, more pertinently, in driving a wedge in their relationship that, I believe, is never fully resolved in their subsequent meetings.

In an equally disturbing fashion, Dr Landau reveals an inconsistency in his willingness to disclose aspects of his life or personality to Ms Alexander. As such, while he is accommodating enough to respond directly and non-defensively to Ms Alexander's comment that he was indiscreet in revealing the name of another of his clients to her (p. 29) and to her observation that he is 'in a bad temper today' (p. 32), his reply to her query as to whether hé is married is to assert '[t]hat's not a question which I would answer' (p. 35). Under the circumstances, I think it would be fair to ask: 'Why not?'

In this instance, Dr Grosjean's (yet another of the various therapists that Ms Alexander meets) words to Ms Alexander could just as easily – and more pertinently – have been directed towards Dr Landau:

> 'There's too much confusion between the professional person and the private individual. You don't know what you're dealing with. And there also seems to be confusion about what you're actually doing with him. It's never been defined, the conditions have never been specified. You don't know what sort of context you're working in.' (p. 83)

For many readers, I imagine, the most disturbing elements regarding Ms Alexander's therapeutic relationship with Dr Landau centre upon their physical encounters which, in some cases, veer towards the sexual. The two protagonists touch, embrace, cuddle and physically attack one another on several occasions. Equally, both acknowledge and express sexual arousal, and each touches the other's genitals. Is such behaviour acceptable in a therapeutic setting? The great majority of therapists would argue that it would not be *unless* the therapist and client were engaged in specific forms of physically-focused, 'body-oriented' therapies such as bioenergetics – which is clearly not the case in this instance. Exceptionally, the psychoanalyst Michael Balint has argued that physical contact between analyst and client might be of therapeutic value when it falls under the confines of 'benign' – rather than 'malignant' – regression on the part of the client (Balint, 1968). Many therapists would question the validity of such distinctions. Nevertheless, even if such could be agreed upon, it is important to note that Balint himself cautions that sexually-focused contact falls under the domain of malignant regression and must be avoided. As such, it would seem that Dr Landau's willingness to allow and engage in physical contact with his client is patently unacceptable.

Recent research on sexual contact between therapists and their clients leaves no doubt that it is psychologically harmful to clients and is a major abuse of the therapist's power and authority (Masson, 1988, 1991; Szymanska and Palmer, 1993). On a related note, I have myself discussed the issue of attraction in the therapeutic encounter and have sought to argue that while attraction (in its varied forms of expression) may be unavoidable, the attentive therapist is clearly capable of dealing with it in a variety of ways which respect the confines of the therapeutic relationship (Spinelli, 1994).

While it is evident that Dr Landau's professional behaviour opens itself to serious criticism on various occasions, I do not wish to overemphasise his specific errors or questionable behaviours, not least because, as readers, we have no access to his version of the events in question. Equally, I can imagine very few, if any, therapists who have not had cause to regret or reconsider interventions they have made at various points in their professional lives. If this view suggests to readers that clients must remain aware that they take risks in entering and remaining in a therapeutic relationship, then they are not mistaken. All relationships – be they familial, romantic, sexual, professional, friendships or whatever – contain risks for their participants. Just as they may be joyous or beneficial, they may also become painful or harmful. It is no different a case for therapeutic relationships. The propagation of the idea that therapeutic relationships can in some way avoid negative possibilities, or are or should be in some sense 'perfect', is both misleading and dangerous and those who perpetuate this view – be they critics or 'evangelical' proponents of therapy – are, at best, naive.

Nevertheless, Ms Alexander's document raises a significant concern. If, as appears to be the case, *every one* of her various encounters with therapists and psychiatrists who represent differing models and approaches to therapy contains troubling elements, is there something specific to therapeutic relationships that tends to dispose them towards unbeneficial consequences? Is there something inherently problematic in the therapeutic encounter?

As a practising therapist, I do not believe this to be the case. However, it does seem to me that certain crucial factors exist in therapy that have not been sufficiently considered by many therapists and that these, in remaining ill-considered, are likely to increase the likelihood of negative or abusively-interpreted experiences.

One important factor that has been drawn to our attention by critics of therapy such as Jeffrey Masson (1988, 1991, 1992) is the issue of *power*. While I agree with Masson that therapists undoubtedly wield power and that, in some circumstances at least, this power is abused, I cannot go along with Masson's conclusion that power *per se* dooms therapy to inevitable abuse. Once again, I have argued elsewhere that *all* relationships are power-based; that in therapy both therapist and client express both similar and differing forms of power, and that, while unavoidable, power, if sufficiently acknowledged and respectfully employed, is not pre-ordained to be problematic (Spinelli, 1994).

Nevertheless, Ms Alexander's text provides obvious testimony which clearly demonstrates how therapist power can be abusive. For instance, consider the meeting she has with a representative of the Institute of Psychoanalysis (pp. 76–8). Recall the informative snippet of dialogue that occurs when, in reply to Ms Alexander's request to help her find another therapist, the representative initially asks her whether she would prefer a male or female therapist. Then, following Ms Alexander's decision that she wants to work with a male therapist, the representative asserts that '[a]t the stage you're at it doesn't make any difference whether it's a man or a woman' (p. 78). Now, why on earth would the representative pretend to want to know Ms Alexander's preference if she has already deigned it to be irrelevant? Further, the manner by which the representative's conclusion is expressed suggests that she (the representative) possesses an understanding of the situation that Ms Alexander does not (cannot?) have and which appears pointless or unnecessary for her to clarify or explain.

Ms Alexander experiences this comment as being 'cryptic' (p. 78). I would view it as an expression of an assumed, if questionable, authority. Such authority seems to me to be derived from the representative's commitment to her theoretical model (in this case, psychoanalysis) which itself allows her to make such pronouncements. This seems to me to be the most pernicious misuse of therapist power. While critics such as Masson have principally focused upon therapists' physical and sexual abuses of power, it seems to me that far more subtle, and devastating, abuses are provoked when therapists are not sufficiently cautious and critical of the theories or models they espouse.

The significance of therapists' uncritical allegiance to, and reliance upon, a particular theoretical model, unfortunately has not been given sufficient attention by the majority of individual therapists or by many of their training institutes. This is a strikingly odd situation, particularly when all available scientific research on this issue concludes that no evidence exists to demonstrate the greater efficacy or outcome success of any one model over any other (Howarth, 1989; Mair, 1992).

If this denouement were not sufficiently disconcerting, it is useful to consider a number of other general conclusions derived from research studies. In spite of numerous attempts to furnish evidence in favour of therapy's most basic and fundamental assumptions regarding such issues as how and why therapy (sometimes) 'works', and what central skills and theoretically and/or experientially derived knowledge-bases form the crucial variables for suitable training of future therapists, the existing data remain uniformly inconclusive (Mair, 1992). Indeed, it appears to be a point of contention as to whether training of any sort is a significant variable in the development of 'good' therapists (Broadbent *et al.*, 1983; Mair, 1992). There is, in fact, so little that one truthfully can state has been scientifically established about either the process or outcomes of therapy that the one reasonably certain conclusion that can be derived from research analyses concerned with the therapeutic process is that it remains a deeply uncertain enterprise.

While it is fair to conclude from research analyses that, in general, therapy tends to promote broadly beneficial outcome consequences in the majority of instances just how such benefits occur remains largely unknown. As one researcher has put it:

> It is now clear from meta-analyses of almost 500 evaluative studies ... that most forms of psychotherapy and counselling are approximately 50 per cent more likely to produce an improvement than would occur without treatment, provided the outcome is assessed from the client's subjective reports. These same meta-analyses mostly fail to show any difference between different forms of treatment, no matter how different in philosophy ... or how different the procedures ... and no matter what the disorder being treated .... The non-specificity of treatment is confirmed by the failure to demonstrate any effect of training on the effectiveness of therapy .... One is driven to the simple conclusion that psychotherapists do not know what they are doing and cannot train others to do it, whatever it is. (Howarth, 1989, p. 150)

In part, this conclusion is likely to be due to the complexity of quantitative and qualitative variables present in any therapeutic encounter which, in themselves, make research a difficult, if not 'impossible' enterprise. Similarly, it may be the case that the research methodologies employed to analyse and evaluate the therapeutic process are, in whole or in part, inadequate (Rowan, 1992). On the other hand, it also remains a possibility that these inconclusive findings point out something which is apparent – if unpalatable: *in spite of what therapists say, they really don't know what they are doing.*

To compound matters further, there also exist significant divergences between what therapists and their clients tend to consider to be the crucial factors determining the success of therapy. While it is typical for therapists to emphasise theory, training and interpretative discourse, clients, on the other hand, point to far more 'prosaic' factors such as simply having the opportunity to talk to and be heard accurately and non-judgementally by their therapist as being the key – even the sole – elements for their experience of beneficial therapy (Howe, 1993).

My own contributions to the debate have sought to demonstrate how the specialist terminology and language of therapy serve to further confound and mystify the process for both therapist and client. Somewhat 'tongue in cheek', I have suggested that in numerous instances, therapists' ungrounded beliefs in their theories act as a kind of 'Dumbo Effect' in that, just like Walt Disney's famous cartoon elephant who believed that he could fly only because he possessed a 'magical' feather, therapists have incorrectly placed their 'faith' in various principles and assumptions that are questionable, unnecessary and, most pertinently, which themselves may be the basis for the various criticisms and concerns raised about therapy (Spinelli, 1994). The psychotherapist John Rowan has succinctly summarised the current state of affairs:

> every single piece of research turns out to be minimally revealing. In each case, whatever variable one looks at, the answer seems to be the same – either there is no effect, or the effect is very small, or the answers are confused in some way. No clear results emerge at all. (Rowan, 1992, p. 162)

> ... it is not OK to say that all therapists are equal: it is much more true to say that we do not know whether they are or not. (Ibid., p. 163).

If therapists were to acknowledge that much of what they assume to be true remains unproven, it might lead them to be far more cautious and hesitant in their statements and interpretations, thereby rectifying at least some of the more questionable assertions of power as witnessed in Ms Alexander's account. In a similar fashion, deprived of their over-reliance upon the truths of their specific theories and models, they might show greater willingness to examine with greater care and attention those more general, or 'non-specific' factors potentially present in all therapies which might well be far more significant and reliable variables influencing beneficial therapeutic encounters and outcomes (Aebi, 1993).

In the pursuit of this tantalising possibility, I, like several other researchers, have concluded that the *one* variable that study after study (for example, Orlinsky and Howard, 1986) singles out as being the crucial factor in all cases of effective therapy turns out to be *the bond that therapists form with their clients.*

Now, while it is evident that most therapists are willing to acknowledge the importance of the establishment and maintenance of a relationship with their clients, there remains a great deal to be done with regard to the study and descriptive analysis of differing types of relationships that can be engendered in therapeutic settings and what, if any, correlations there may exist between these and the client's experience of beneficial interventions. For example, one researcher has concluded that:

> It seems that the amount of improvement noted by a patient in psychotherapy is highly correlated with his attitudes to the therapist .... More important, the therapist's warmth, his respect and interest ... emerged as important ingredients in the amount of

change reported ... the more uncertain the patient felt about the therapist's attitude toward him, the less change he tended to experience. (Strupp *et al.*, 1969, p. 77)

While another has suggested, somewhat more caustically, that

[therapists] do seem to be able to help people; perhaps because they often manage to outgrow the handicaps imposed by their training. (Mair, 1992, p. 152)

In a similar fashion, a number of existentially-informed practitioners have emphasised the importance of the meeting, or *encounter*, between therapist and client and have examined what it might mean for the therapist to attempt to 'be with and for' the client (Laing, 1960; May, 1967; van Deurzen-Smith, 1988; Spinelli, 1989, 1994). This shift in emphasis away from the specific application of learned skills and techniques ('doing') and towards encounter ('being') has been shown to instigate immediate repercussions for the therapist insofar as he or she must be both willing (and at least to some extent able) to explore and acknowledge what he or she brings to the encounter and how such influences, biases and assumptions come into play at the various self/other levels of relating with the client. This is no easy task to attempt, not least because it can, and often does, provoke confrontation with the therapist's own unwillingness to listen and/or attend to the client in a direct and open manner.

If the emphasis upon 'doing' expresses a focus upon specific factors, it is arguable that the exploration of the 'being' qualities of encounter may allow a more detailed analysis and understanding of crucial nonspecific factors in the therapeutic process. Perhaps, if therapists acknowledged their uncertainties with regard to what they 'do' and were to begin a more careful and systematic exploration of the intersubjective qualities expressed through their self/other encounters with their clients, then, paradoxically, they might gain valuable clues leading to the clarification of so many of the unanswered (and seemingly unanswerable) questions of therapy.

Earlier, I referred to the therapeutic relationship between Ms Alexander and Dr Landau as being 'a tragedy'. I believe this to be so because, in spite of the many troubling aspects in their relationship, there also seem to be moments of genuine encounter between them.

'I'm able to leave you because I know that you're not abandoning me ...'
'No, I'm not abandoning you.' (p. 24–5)

'If I wasn't going away I'd stay with you,' I said hesitantly.

'You'd stay with me.' He repeated my words gently as if he was touched by what I had said.

Nothing was said for a while.

'With Dr Weissmann I only wanted his body, but you, I want all of you.'

As I said this it seemed like the most intimate thing I had ever communicated to anyone. (p. 24)

Contrast these comments with earlier ones concerning Ms Alexander's relationship with Dr Weissmann:

...[P]ride prevented me saying a lot of things to him which should have been said .... (p. 10)

...[T]he superficiality of the relationship ... was clearly indicated by the fact that although my mother died during the period I was seeing him, we never discussed it. I felt that it would be an affront to my mother to talk about her with this man. (p. 16)

As the representative from the Institute of Psychoanalysis so succinctly summarises the issue: 'Well ... there has to be a certain minimum amount of confidence if the relationship is to work ...'. (p. 78)

Given that Ms Alexander felt such a lack of confidence in so many of her therapeutic encounters, or alternatively, experienced it only briefly in her relationship with Dr Landau, a final, necessary question remains to be asked: why did she continue in therapy? Indeed, why do these encounters continue to maintain such a powerful hold upon her life? Her own answer, as supplied throughout the text, focuses upon the idea of an 'unbroken transference'. Is this the most fruitful explanation?

'Transference' refers to the hypothesis that various forms of emotions and attitudinal reactions felt towards 'significant others' in a client's life (such as one's parents) are expressed in the therapeutic relationship in that they are attributed to, or 'transferred onto' the therapist. As Dr Landau explains at one point:

'My actual person doesn't count in all this. I can represent your father, your mother, or anything else at all. It doesn't matter.' (p. 22)

While principally employed by psychoanalysts, the idea of transference has been accepted (at least in a general sense) by a wide range of psychotherapies. Nevertheless, as a number of therapists have pointed out, it remains an idea that is both unproven and which is open to significant critiques.

It is important to be clear, for example, that transference is the hypothetical cause to the observable phenomena of a client's emotional arousal towards the therapist. However, many therapists seem to have failed to understand this distinction and have erroneously assumed that the observed phenomena and the transference hypothesis are one and the same. That clients can and do experience strong emotions towards their therapists is beyond doubt; that .the source of these emotions is best explained via transference, however, remains an open question.

One important critic of the hypothesis of transference, John Shlien, has argued the case for a 'countertheory of transference' which suggests that '[t]ransference is a fiction, invented and maintained by the therapist to protect himself from the consequences of his own behaviour' (Shlien, 1984, p. 153). Alternatively, it can also be argued that transference allows therapists to distance themselves – and their own perceptions, emotions, issues and concerns – from the impact of direct, sometimes highly emotional, encounters with their clients. In other words, transference can be seen to be a hypothetical construct principally designed to defend or protect the therapist from acknowledging or considering the possible meaning of the client's emotional reaction towards him or her as an expression of the client's experience of the current relationship (that is, that between the client and the therapist). This, initially 'heretical', idea helps to explain why, for instance, there is often little agreement between therapists as to when a client's responses are judged to be 'transferential'.

On reflection, if clients come into contact, perhaps for the first time in their lives, with a figure of authority who expresses respect, concern, and attentive care towards them, who treats their accounts of their experiences as meaningful, and who appears to understand and accept them,

> is it *so* surprising that they should experience gratitude, deep trust, affection, love and fear of separation towards that person? And, in the same way, if the clients had come to believe that that figure of authority had offered respect and interest but, in fact, had betrayed them by not believing their accounts or siding with other versions of the accounts, or misinterpreting them, would it equally be surprising if they responded angrily or violently towards the therapist? (Spinelli, 1994, p. 186)

As Shlien points out, therapists' attempted entry into the worldviews of their clients is a form of 'love-making' (whether intended or not), just as the failure to enter, or misunderstanding, is a form of 'hate-making'.

I enjoin readers to go back to those sections of Ms Alexander's text where notions of transference are invoked and to reconsider these in the light of what has just been argued. I think that they will find sufficient reason to question the transference 'explanations' suggested.

But if it is not transference, then what keeps Ms Alexander 'stuck' in her state? I would suggest that Ms Alexander experienced therapy's potential 'offering' to be part of a human and humane meeting, or encounter, between individuals – an encounter which allows the client to explore and clarify and challenge him- or herself in a respectful, attentive and honest manner which reflects not only the therapist's stance toward the client, but, just as significantly, the client's stance towards him or herself. I believe that Ms Alexander caught 'glimpses' of this potential in several of her meetings with therapists – glimpses which remained sufficiently powerful and significant to keep her wanting to go back, but which, through her therapists' misuse of their authority (through ignorance, arrogance, fear, and/or over-reliance upon questionable theoretically-derived assumptions), also remained fleeting and which, ultimately, dissolved, leaving her only with discontent and understandable anger. That this may have been a recurrent 'theme' in Ms Alexander's life does not reduce the impact of her therapists' false offerings. We have no need to invoke mystificatory terms like transference to make substantial sense of her ongoing dilemma.

As a practising psychotherapist who remains convinced of the beneficial potentials of therapy, I can only express sadness and regret that Ms Alexander's experience – like that of a significant number of other individuals – was so clearly negative. I hope that, in writing about it, she has found some means both to come to terms with it and to move on in her life. More to the point, I harbour the hope that her account will at least have the positive impact of challenging therapists to address the issues raised in an honest and non-defensive manner so that we will all – therapists and clients alike – benefit from such.

Clearly, such a step will require a good deal of courage and tenacity on the part of therapists regardless of which model or theory they espouse. Even so, it asks no more of us than that which we request of our clients.

REFERENCES

Aebi, J. (1993) 'Nonspecific and specific factors in therapeutic change among different approaches to counselling', *Counselling Psychology Review* 8(3): 19–32.

Balint, M. (1968) *The Basic Fault*. London: Tavistock.

Broadbent, J., Day, A., Khaleelee, O., Miller, E. and Pym, D. (1983) *Psychotherapists and the Process of Profession-Building*. London: OPUS.

Crews, F. (1995) 'Cheerful assassin defies analysis', *Times Higher Educational Supplement*, 3 March 1995, pp. 20–1.

Afterword

Howarth, I. (1989) 'Psychotherapy: who benefits?', *The Psychologist*, 2(4): 149–52.

Howe, D. (1993) *On Being A Client: understanding the process of counselling and psychotherapy*. London: Sage.

Laing, R. D. (1960) *The Divided Self*. London: Tavistock.

Mair, K. (1992) 'The myth of therapist expertise', *Psychotherapy and its Discontents* (W. Dryden and C. Feltham, eds). Milton Keynes: Open University Press.

Masson J. (1988) *Against Therapy: emotional tyranny and the myth of psychological healing*. London: Fontana (1989).

—— (1991) *Final Analysis: the making and unmaking of a psycho-analyst*. London: HarperCollins (1992).

—— (1992) 'The myth of psychotherapy', *Psychotherapy and its Discontents* (W. Dryden and C. Feltham, eds). Milton Keynes: Open University Press.

May, R. (1967) *Psychology and the Human Dilemma*. New York: Norton.

Orlinsky, D. E. and Howard, K. I. (1986) 'Process and outcome in psychotherapy', *Handbook of Psychotherapy and Behaviour Change* (3rd edn, S. L. Garfield and A. E. Bergin, eds). New York: Wiley.

Rowan, J. (1992) 'Response to K. Mair's "The myth of therapist expertise"', *Psychotherapy and its Discontents* (W. Dryden and C. Feltham, eds). Milton Keynes: Open University Press.

Shlien, J. M. (1984) 'A countertheory of transference', *Client Centered Therapy and the Person Centered Approach* (R. Levant and J. Shlien, eds). New York: Praeger.

Spinelli, E. (1989) *The Interpreted World: and introduction to phenomenological psychology*. London: Sage.

—— (1994) *Demystifying Therapy*. London: Constable.

Strupp, H., Fox, R. and Lessler, K. (1969) *Patients View Their Psychotherapy*. Baltimore, MD: Johns Hopkins University Press.

Szymanska, K. and Palmer, S. (1993) 'Therapist–client sexual contact', *Counselling Psychology Review* 8(4): 22–33.

Townsend, C. (1993) 'What's in a name?', *Counselling*, 4: 252.

van Deurzen-Smith, E. (1988) *Existential Counselling in Practice*. London: Sage.

Dr Ernesto Spinelli is a practising UKCP registered existential psychotherapist, BAC accredited counsellor and a BPS Chartered Counselling Psychologist. He is Principal Lecturer at the School of Psychotherapy and Counselling, Regent's College, London. He is the current Chair of the Society for Existential Analysis and author of two books, *The Interpreted World: an introduction to phenomenological psychology* (Sage: 1989) and *Demystifying Therapy* (Constable, 1994) and many journal papers and articles dealing with the theory and practise of therapy.